CONCILIUM

concilium

1992/4

WHERE IS GOD? A CRY OF HUMAN DISTRESS

Edited by

Christian Duquoc and
Casiano Floristan

SCM Press Ltd
London

August 1992

ISBN: 0334 03015 3

Typeset at The Spartan Press Ltd, Lymington, Hants
Printed and bound in Great Britain by
Mackays of Chatham PLC, Chatham, Kent

Concilium: Published February, April, June, August, October, December

Contents

Editorial

Where is God? The question might seem to be an idle one, since God escapes our experience, and we ceaselessly look for signs of his action or his presence. However, it is a crucial question, since already in the Bible it reveals impatience, rebellion, resignation or crazy hope. And it is a topical question, since now that they have been liberated from God's social attestation by the churches, our contemporaries cannot assign any official abode to God and therefore become either indifferent or anxious, and on rare occasions aggressive. From now on it would seem vain to kill God like the scatterbrains of whom Nietzsche speaks in his parable of the crazy ones.

Where is God? The import of the question has been changed: and that is what the first article is about. I have not organized it on the basis of a history of ideas but by taking up the traumas produced by the tragic way in which the New World was discovered, traumas which even now underlie the problems tackled by liberation theology. The cry of the psalmist is no stranger to these problems, as can be seen from the article by E. Gerstenberger. However, the question has to be put in the harsh setting of everyday life: Gregory Baum does this on the basis of his personal experience, for those who cry to God from the depth of their sickness; Pablo Richard describes how the suffering and humiliation of women make this question 'Where is God?' quite specific; A. Tornos reminds us that all human beings are overwhelmed by guilt, whether real or imaginary, and that in spite of this they try to encounter the face of the merciful God. Finally, P. de Locht brings out the final distress, death, as the place where, without support, in the night, absolute trust is given.

This everyday confrontation makes the question a radical one, a topic for philosophy as well as theology, pointing towards the mystical. Yves Cattin, on a broad scale, has discussed this topic from a particular, apparently anodyne perspective: the metaphor of God. Something else is evoked there without the void being removed. It is left to Isabelle Chareire to designate the church as the body which raises this question in the paradoxical situation of its visible form: it can do so with honesty, avoiding either scorning the institution or exalting it. Personal distress, philosophical and theological questions and church paradoxes still leave space for reflection: on the messianisms and hopes raised by the biblical link with God, although this link has been secularized. Courageously, G. Faus, in an up-to-date setting, tells us what is at stake in this question in both religious and political terms. Thus the end sees a return to what was evoked at the beginning: the relevance of the reference point given by liberation theologies, but also the limitations of their metamorphosis into theologies of history.

Christian Duquoc OP

'Who is God?' becomes 'Where is God?' The Shift in a Question

Christian Duquoc

'What is God?' asks Luther in his *Greater Catechism*. 'God,' he replies, 'is one from whom we must expect all good and in whom we can take refuge in all our needs. So that to have a God is nothing else than to believe in him with all our hearts. Trust and faith of the heart alone make both God and idol. If the faith and trust are right, then your God is also the right God, and again, if your trust is false and wrong then you do not have the right God. For faith and God hold close together. Whatever your heart clings to and relies upon is properly your God.'[1]

For me, this text from Luther evokes the debate which was unfolding at that time in another cultural arena: the debate being carried on by Las Casas in defence of the Indians.

Las Casas had denounced precisely and vigorously the injustice of the conquest of the 'Western Indies'. He had described the atrocities, cruelties and crimes to which they had been delivered up by the Conquistadors. He ceaselessly informed the Spanish Crown of the responsibility that it would incur if it did not do something about the brutality of the soldiers. Anyone could assess the terrible effects of the conquest: forced labour, bringing about the deaths of whole populations. There were thinkers and theologians who justified the Conquest, set it within the divine plan, seeing it as the necessary cost of conversion. They argued that in fact the Indians, by their crimes and their idolatry, deserved this treatment, even if some excesses should have been corrected. The major sign of their perversity was to be found in their cultic practices: sacrificing human beings to their gods. This was one of the topics of the discussion between Las Casas and Sepulveda at Velladolid in 1550: were human sacrifices the effect of a diabolic faith? What kind of God did they reveal?

Las Casas defended the following thesis: God is the one to whom one offers the best that one has. Nothing is of greater value than human life. The sacrificial offering of this to God bears witness to the intensity of the religious fervour of the Indians. Beyond question they are wrong, but this objective error is in no way to the detriment of the magnitude of their feelings and their idea of the majesty of God. Even if they are wrong about the identity of God, they are certainly not mistaken about the feelings that one should have for him. So Las Casas would have subscribed to the definition of God put forward by Luther: 'The one from whom we should expect all good and in whom we can take refuge in all our needs.' Even more radical is Luther's expression, 'Trust and faith make both God and idol.' This expression illuminates Las Casas' option: the Conquistadors who claim to announce the true God prove by their acts that they have no God other than their cupidity, indicated by their thirst for God. In fact they have no other God than their perverse desire, to which they sacrifice the Indians. By contrast, the Indians who sacrifice human beings renounce their cupidity: they offer to the God in whom they trust what they think to be their best. So the objectively true God of the Conquistadors is no more than an idol, a metaphor of their cupidity. The objectively false God of the Indians is a true God, since he opens their desire to that which is beyond themselves. God is defined by the truth of the desire, and paradoxically, he proves to be true where he is objectively said to be false. The upheaval of the conquest of the New World, like the upheaval of the Reformation, posed dangerous questions to the certainties which had come down through the ages: the objectivity of God, i.e. the reality of God in itself, duly signified in language, is not the guarantee of his truth for us. Assurance about his identity ceases, and the fine constructions which denote him turn out in practice to be false. So who is God that he can be so pliable? Would there not be more justification in looking for a place where he acts, since his identity and his essence support contradictory historical functions? This question defines the course of this article: abstract identity, the impossibility of locating God, the imperfect witness.

1. Abstract identity

God does not give himself in experience; he announces himself in witnesses. Scripture tells us that the universe points to his power and his divinity, and that human beings did not want to recognize him:

> For the wrath of God is revealed from heaven against all ungodliness and wickedness of men who by their wickedness suppress the truth, For

what can be known about God is plain to them, because God has shown it to them. Ever since the creation of the world his invisible nature, namely, his eternal power and deity, have been clearly perceived in the things that have been made. So they are without excuse: for although they knew God, they did not honour him as God or give thanks to him' (Rom. 1.18–21).

The prophets, too, tried to do away with error or indifference. At the beginning of this trend, Moses' vision represents a break: God gives his Name as a guarantee of his liberating action (Ex. 3.14). Deutero-Isaiah takes over this procedure in the Book of Consolation (Isa. 40–55): Israel must put its trust in the one whom no power can thwart. He is the God of Abraham, Isaac and Jacob. Nothing defines his identity or his essence except the action which he takes within a framework which he has fixed, the covenant, and a promise which opens up the present to the future in a positive way. This discretion about God's identity does not disappear in the New Testament. The question which Philip puts to Jesus betrays the impatience of his desire to see God: 'Lord, will you show us the Father?' (John 14.8). This desire cannot be fulfilled, since no one has ever seen God (John 1.18). Even if the only begotten Son has revealed him (John 1.18), and to see Jesus is to see the Father (John 14.8), it nevertheless remains the case that God in himself evades our experience; the death of Jesus on the cross seals this inability to know God.

This discretion explains the constantly repeated concern in Christian history to unmask the identity of God. The question 'Who is he?' is transformed into the question 'What is he?' Luther's Greater Catechism which I quoted at the beginning opens with the question 'What is God?' This shift from the identity expressed in naming God towards the essence articulated in the definition is amazing. The shift does not come about without a reversal: the essence of God is no longer on the side of objectivity but on that of desire. As if the tension over grasping the object had been too frustrating, the theologian turns towards the desire, reckoning that this presence which can be found in experience is a protection against wanting to have access to the mastery of an identity which slips away. This procedure breaks with the constantly renewed desire to designate 'who God is' by means of a definition of his essence. In reality preaching and theology have only picked off sequences of attributes or qualities where God is concerned: God is immutable, impassible, eternal, good, omnipotent, infinite, etc . . . The accumulation of qualities in no way changes our inability to grasp God's essence, and God's identity does not cease to evade epistemological procedures. When such a way of thinking believes that it has at last reached God, it vanishes in the dust of words, or has illusions about its power of knowledge. There is no answer to the question 'Who is God?', since every answer slips away into abstraction. We, too, are referred to the witness who dares to say that to see him is to see God, at the very moment when grasping his tangible body puts us at a distance from the One whom no experience can appropriate. Beyond question, in a scholarly and even catechetical tradition, everything conspires to give to words indicating that there is no possibility of defining God a power that they do not have. In this way God is objectivized; everyone knows who he is and what he is. One can also act in his name, require the newly discovered Indians to recognize him. The upheaval brought about by the Conquest as much achieved this objective and, in the last resort, mercantile availability of God as Luther's preaching undermined the Roman claim to speak and decide in his name. In denouncing gold as the object of the Conquistadors' desires, Las Casas made unreal and thus vain their claim to be advancing into unknown territory in the name of the Christian God. They failed to recognize his identity, since he was not present in their desire. Their objective knowledge of the identity of this Christian God did not engender any worthy practice, but their effective practice, their greedy desire, revealed the identity of their God.

The question of God's identity or the definition of his essence outside this desire is a false one. The Indian paradox of the intensity of their veneration of God in the absolute of human sacrifice revealed the point at which 'true knowledge' did not matter very much. So the question is no longer one of knowing 'who God is' or 'what God is' but of discerning where God acts. Certainly not, de Las Casas thinks, where the Conquistadors massacred the Indians in the name of the Christian God. Certainly not, Luther proclaims, in pontifical Rome, where corruption reigns. The question of the identity of God and of the definition of his essence has lost its relevance because it has subsisted, in its abstract eternity, in the midst of criminal practices. It is more worthwhile to discern where God acts than to know who he is. The knowledge of his identity does not free people from idolatry.

2. The impossibility of locating God

The traditional witnesses are dying away: they have claimed to know the identity of God, they have asserted that they knew who he was, they have wrongly and erroneously invoked his name and have brought about nothing but destruction. They have deluded themselves over the effects of their knowledge. God is not where they put him. His residence is elsewhere. The experience of the Conquest with its train of atrocities shifts the location of God; he is not where people claim that he is. The traumatism of the Reformation exiles him from the institution which was the guarantee of his action: he no longer has an abode. Those who were convinced that they were acting in his name because they knew who and what he was have led the people astray. The history that they direct and abuse no longer points towards the Christian God. Where is his place from now on, since his identity has not preserved him from exile? Must 'the heavens tell of his glory', as Psalm 18 has it, or must one cease to attempt to give him an abode?

The revolution connected with Galileo which took place in cosmology, where hitherto interactions between the divine and the universe tied in well with each other, robbed God of his abode in heaven. The universe obeys mathematical laws and is intelligible, but in moving the earth from the centre and suggesting that the anthropocentrism of the universe is simply paranoia, the new cosmology created a distance between God and his dynamism. Did he perhaps give the initial flick to this great system which is constantly on the move? There is no need to appeal to him in order to make it intelligible. God no longer has a dwelling place in this world, and if the heavens tell of his glory, they do so posthumously. One can understand Pascal when he says that 'infinite space is terrifying'. The subsequent intervention of the universe has not assuaged this anxiety. The universe in its movement is indifferent to human destiny. There is no longer any connection between its future and our collective future. J. Rostand has given emotive expression to this situation, which is at once both new and tragic. He writes of the human race swept away in the death of the solar system:

> What point will it have reached on its spiritual curve when it allows itself to be buried for ever in an icy shroud? What will have been its achievements and its exploits? Will it have given its all, exhausted all its dreams, fulfilled its supreme destiny? Or will it be submerged in full flood, in the youth of promises and hopes?
>
> A derisory atom lost in the inert and boundless cosmos, man knows that his feverish activity is only a small local phenomenon, ephemeral, without meaning and without a goal. He knows that his values are values for him alone, and that from an astronomical perspective the fall of an empire, or even the ruin of an ideal, does not count any

more than the crushing of an ant-hill under the feet of a heedless passer-by.[2]

In this lamentation we hear something of the delirium of the madman reported by Nietzsche. Brandishing a lantern at noon, he cried incessantly, 'I seek God.' Hilarious bystanders joked: 'Have you lost him? Is he hiding somewhere? Has he emigrated?' And the madman asks, 'Where is God?'[3]

I shall ignore the theme of his assassination here – it is the metaphor of his exile. The universe has become uninhabited. The Psalmist already heard the ironical accusation of the enemies of Israel: 'Where is now your God?' However, at that time the universe was inhabited, peopled by gods, though the One on whom Israel called had gone into exile.

The time of the conquest of America shattered the illusion that the actions of those who knew and rehearsed the identity of God were the concrete expression of his will in this world. Las Casas had denounced the perversity of this interpretation. At that time God had removed himself from the conquering history, since he had gone into exile from a universe whose destiny has no common measure with ours. It is useless to ask who he is, but a matter of urgency to establish where he is. To know where he is amounts to discerning his action. For a long time people believed that those who laid claim to God's name were fulfilling his actions. Fractures were produced; from now on, no institution, not even any ecclesiastical institution, could be sure of housing God. God no longer had any official address. We too have become nomads again. Where is God?

The Christian is no less plagued by this question than the non-believer. Our recent history is peopled by men and women seeking signs of where God is. But spatial metaphors would already seem outmoded. Perhaps temporal metaphors would be more appropriate? The introduction of the category of 'signs of the times' is a response to this expectation: since it is no longer possible to say where God is, perhaps his action can be perceived in a dynamic of transformation. Everyone will remember the success of the 'signs of the times' at the Second Vatican Council: social movements like decolonization and women's liberation were said to denote the action of God in our time. In his encyclical *Redemptoris Missio*, John Paul II writes:

> Thus the Spirit, who 'blows where he wills' (John 3.8), who 'was already at work in the world before Christ was glorified', and who 'has filled the world . . ., holds all things together (and) knows what is said' (Wisdom 1.7) leads us to broaden our vision in order to ponder his activity in every time and place.[4]

We are invited to see the action which transforms. From now on the question 'Where is God?' relates to religious or ecclesiastical movements in the world which give some indication that the Spirit is working in them. There is no longer any question of locating God; there is no longer any institution which shelters God with any certainty. Events furnish signs. It is necessary to discern their meaning, follow their orientation, flow with them. There is no longer any place where God dwells; it is from events that the provisional action of the Spirit shines forth. Thus we are directed towards witnesses, the agents of these events.

3. The imperfect witness

Those who claimed to state the identity of God have come to grief: they have inscribed in our history a social reality which runs counter to their knowledge. So it is evident that it was not enough to proclaim God as 'that than which no greater can be conceived'.[5] The effect produced was not up to the level of the announcement or the proclamation. It was not enough even to abandon the objectivity of God and substitute religious fervour or intensity for it: inscribing this reversal of perspective on history did not banish violence. In this brief account it would be out of place to follow the ups and downs of the theories of the objectivity of God to the point when they became devalued in Kantian philosophy. Beyond question there is a link between the future of the question of God in modern philosophy, the dedivinization of the universe by science and the historical failure of Christianity to produce a society in conformity with its ideal. If the question 'Who is God?' has become secondary to the question 'Where is God?', and if finally the question 'Where is God?' is posed for the moment in the effort of discerning God's active presence in events, any seizure of God is a vain enterprise: there is a constant distance between him and those who proclaim him. They have not been able to define his identity further, any more than they have been able to assign him an abode, to do away with the ambivalence of events and cry at last, 'God is here!' God has no identity card, God has no home, God has no historical actions peculiar to him. So where is he to be located?

One 'incident' reported by Elie Wiesel can guide our researches. The scene takes place in a Nazi concentration camp. Jews are forced by the SS to watch the hanging of a young boy. Many among them pray for God to deliver him. Nothing happens. Then one of them cries, 'Where is God?' Another replies, 'He is there, on the gallows.'

Christians cannot read this account unmoved. They remember what happened to Jesus: he was hung on the cross. And when he saw that his prayer was not heard, he cried out, 'My God, my God, why have you forsaken me?' (Mark 15.34). According to the evangelist Mark, these were his last words. But like an unexpected echo, the centurion present says, 'Truly, this man was the Son of God' (Mark 15.39). Jesus, hung on the cross and abandoned by God, is identified by this pagan. God was with him, where he was dying. In his very exclusion, Jesus, cast out by all – the religious powers, the political powers, the mob – at the gates of the city, is an indication of the presence of God. A few of the faithful recognize him. Where is God? He is there even when Jesus dies, rejected.

Those who seek God come up against this paradox: the knowledge of his identity, the effort to read events, the attempt to assign him to an institution, tend to come about outside this original event, the cross. However, new thoughts, based on precise practices, come to be expressed. God is where the poor, the outcast, the scorned, are to be found. God is where one would not expect him. In the sixteenth century, a disciple of Las Casas, Felipe Gueman Poma de Ayala, wrote, 'Faith clearly shows us that where we find the poor, the martyred Indian, there is Jesus Christ, for in Jesus Christ God made himself truly poor.' The first witness of God in the world is the one who has no place there. This is not a witness by word or knowledge. God is in him because he is nothing. Independently of the question of justice, the option of liberation theology for the poor is a theologal decision for the indication of God in this world. Where is God? He is not among those who know his identity, he is not in the institutions which represent him; he is precisely where no one expects him: the one who has nothing is his abode and points to him.

'The idea of the localization of the divine is vital: to recognize, to denote the divine, is to give it limits without which it would be submerged in all creation; in fact, before the erection of the tabernacle the Word of God came forth and entered the dwelling places of the people of the world who had been petrified with fear, cf. Tanh.Teruma 9.'[6] The New Testament moved the location of God by shifting his abode from the temple to the body of Jesus. But he is the very one who dies on the cross, outcast. The outcast is from henceforth a pointer to the presence of God. This does not mean that the outcast is a perfect witness; but he is an indication that this world is not the kingdom of God, he is that outside our societies which asks them about their organization and their goal; he represents their potential subversion. Where is God? He is where a concrete being points to the kingdom which has not come; he is where a concrete being vitiates the claim of our society to fulfil all desires. To locate God with the outcasts, of whom the poor are the major representatives, does not say anything about the holiness of the poor, but the poor do represent him as prophets against our closed and unjust societies. This localization emerges as a focal point; any action which breaks down the bounds of exclusion and poverty is related to the action of the Spirit. The 'signs of the times' fall in with this interpretation. As for the institutional church, it indicates where God is to the degree that it works to throw back the frontiers of exclusion and poverty, and also to the degree that it shows itself to be a prophet for our societies on the basis of the cross of Christ.

The shift in the locating of God recognized in the universe and history does not imply that this world is stripped of its value: it remains under the divine blessing declared in the book of Genesis. That God's identity escapes us because his name resists all magical usage, that his abode is restricted to the poor and the outcast, is no condemnation of the world. On the contrary, as the Midrash quoted above suggests, it is this withdrawal which incites humanity to take God's cause in hand. But this withdrawal stops at the precise point where the movement of history overwhelms men and women. God is then with them. And he gives a sign of being with them. The God who withdraws so as not to overwhelm his creatures with his power sets up his tent where all hope seems to have been abolished. I cannot find a better way of ending than to quote a text of Rashi on Deut. 32 and the commentary which Marauni gives on it:

'God is led to show his love towards Israel in the same way as the eagle which is full of tenderness for its little ones; the eagle does not enter its nest brutally, but first beats and flaps its wings above the nest so that the eaglets wake up and have the strength to welcome it. The eagle flies over its little ones; without pressing heavily upon them it glides, touching them and not touching them.' The *tohu wabohu*, the separation between the waters above and below (which prefigures the separation between heaven and earth) manifests this distance that the creator puts between himself and his creation in order to safeguard its autonomy. Without it, the world would be 'overwhelmed' by the divine, absorbed into it: the *tohu wabohu* resides in creation, since through it the world distinguishes itself from the divine and gives itself a place as creature. However, its distance from the creator should not be understood as an absolute separation, since that would detach the world radically from the creator. In fact it is only virtual ('two to three fingers') and paradoxical. It is 'supposed' and cannot be thought.[7]

God has set up his tabernacle among us in Jesus in such a way that his majesty does not overwhelm his people. This habitat has been excluded from the world. The poor and the outcast are his present abode. So his divinity enquires, but does not impose itself. At the time of the birth of Jesus to Joseph and Mary, Luke reminds us that 'there was no room for them at the inn' (2.7). God is always outside, with those whom the course of the world casts out there.

Translated by John Bowden

Notes

1. Luther, 'The Greater Catechism', Part 1, on the First Commandment, in *Luther's Primary Works*, ed. H. Wace and C. A. Buchheim, London 1896.
2. J. Rostand, *L'homme*, Paris 1962, 172–3.
3. F. Nietzsche, *The Gay Science*, 3, 125.
4. John-Paul II, *Redemptoris Missio*, 29.
5. Anselm of Canterbury, *Proslogion*, 2.
6. Midrash Rabba I, Genesis Rabba, Commentary by Bernard Marauni, Bereshit V, p. 79, Paris 1987.
7. Ibid., 54.

'Where is God?' The Cry of the Psalmists

Erhard S. Gerstenberger

1. God's absence today

Is there such a thing as 'modern' man, who simply wants to be his own master? Who right to the depths of his being indifferently contemplates an empty universe with which he can enter only into a technical relationship? Or is 'modern' man someone who has denied God and who – tormented by guilt feelings and inferiority complexes – has to live out his delusion of omnipotence in compensation?[1] Who is this enlightened, modern man?

Seeking to define present-day people does not get us very far. Our world society is too multifarious; the traditions of faith are too different, as are the experiences of millions of people on all the continents. There is no one type of person. However, one thing can be said quite definitely: there are experiences of God in all the cultures and religions of this earth. And where God is present, there can also be the shock of God's absence. Can anything be said today about this remoteness of God?

People experience God mediated by their environment. The mystical ways of the knowledge of God are a communion with being; as such, they also presuppose the world. As always, in the midst of the technological world as in the hinterland, the 'absence of God' is produced by circumstances and effects.

Need teaches us not only to pray but also to curse. Where people vegetate in extreme poverty and under the pressure of unspeakable suffering, as in Third World countries and at the socially weakest levels of industrial countries, the elemental experience of godforsakenness also breaks through. The miracle takes place, and believing communities come into being in shanty towns and slum settlements. And the natural, human thing also happens: despair advances. An Argentinian song goes:

One day I asked, 'Grandfather, where is God?'
My grandfather became sad and did not give me an answer.
My grandfather died in the fields, without prayer or confession.
The Indios buried him, to the music of flute and drum.[2]

In the following verses the question is put to the father: he, too, knows no answer and dies a godforsaken death. The singer is reluctant to ask his brother, of the same generation, for God is certainly not with the oppressed forester in the mountains, but is sitting at the businessman's table. God is concerned with the possibilities of life, with basic welfare on this earth. If the means of survival are chronically lacking, generation by generation, then belief in God's providence must go astray. Or a process of purging must be devised to explain the deprivations and the impossibility of living a full span of life, interpreting it as the pledge of betterment in another life. Or the result must simply become apathy, without speech or thought, at most an attitude still capable of finding somewhere the crumbs which allow the light of life to flicker on. I can picture the Brazilian *nordestinos* (day-labourers in the sugar-cane growing areas of the north-east), dried up by sun and hunger, living signs of the absence of God.

It is not hunger alone which makes people despair. Loss of rights, violation of human dignity and persecution weigh at least as heavily. In our supposedly enlightened twentieth century, contempt for human beings has swelled like an avalanche. As a German I think first of all of the annihilation of the Jewish people in Europe, of labour camps and crematorium ovens during Hitler's rule. Millions of victims had to nurse their doubts about God's righteousness in the horror of the ghetto and the machinery of killing. Anyone who could still sing hymns in Auschwitz, which people actually did, needed more than human strength. Even those with the strongest faith experienced God's absence at least temporarily in the senseless hatred and murder. Izabela Gelbard put experiences from the Warsaw ghetto into poetry:

Mother and old woman and defenceless girl,
protected by the holy hands of our fathers,
who during the slaughter, in blood and cursing,
called to their God, 'LORD, YOU are our protection . . .'

But he did not protect – he was not in the ghetto,
probably the shame of it choked him.
Even Szaja Judkiewicz perished. Who was he,
Judkiewicz? An old, pious Jewish man.[3]

The poet sets the unshakable faith of the ninety-four-year-old man against despair in God.

> O Adonai! Without shroud, without *tefillin* (prayer thong),
> forgive me, forgive me, YOU are great, LORD OF GRACE.
> YOUR mercy embraces me, YOUR mercy surrounds me,
> although I am without *tallis* (prayer shawl), which the enemy
> trampled on.[4]

Quite apart from the indescribable Holocaust of the Hitler period, there have been countless victims around the earth. On the Indian reserves, in labour camps and countless torture chambers and prisons, among enslaved women workers, in the theatres of war and among the endless streams of refugees in our times, cries have been uttered for the God who has disappeared, cries full of bitterness and despair.

Where else does the question of God arise in our time? We would be ill-advised to see only the material and social occasions. The spiritual, enlightened legacy of the past century which has now brewed up in science and technology is similarly the root for radical and desperate questioning. Is the universe cold and void? Is there a chance of putting a stop to *homo faber*? Is he in process of taking all creative power into his hands?

Where is God in the modern cultural world of gene manipulation and space flights? Literature, theatre, films – right down to the genre of science fiction and science horror strips – have taken up the theme. Among physicists in modern times there have always been those who have held firm to the notion of a creator (like Albert Einstein, Niels Bohr and so on). Other Western scientists speak, in the light of Jewish-Christian creation faith, of an anthropic universe, i.e. a universe orientated on human beings and their knowledge and understanding.[5] Yet others reject the existence of any deity: they claim that this cannot be reconciled with the laws of physics. The knowable universe functions without the hypothesis of a divine creation or guidance. 'The old covenant is broken; man finally knows that he is alone in the unfeeling expanses of the universe from which he emerged by chance. Nowhere is either his lot or his duty written down.'[6] Here, apparently, all questions about God end.

2. The Psalms and us

Of the 150 prayers and songs in the Old Testament Psalter, about 40 belong to the category of 'individual laments'. They reflect the personal distress of people whose life is in danger. Serious illness, social scorn, evil circumstances, unexplained misfortunes and anxieties have them in their grasp, heralds of death and the powers of the underworld. The depths, the 'maw', reach out for them or seem already to have swallowed them up.

> I sink in deep mire;
> where there is no foothold.
> I have come into deep water,
> and the flood sweeps over me.
> I am weary with my crying;
> my throat is parched.
> My eyes grow dim
> with waiting for my God (Ps. 69.2–4; cf. Ps. 88.5–7; 130.1;
>   Jonah 2.3–7).

The distress cannot be explained by chance, blind fate or some mechanical causes. The deity is involved in the threat to life in some still unknown way. The sufferer needs rapid help; his family sends for the healer or man of God (cf. I Kings 14.2f.; II Kings 1.2; 4.22). Only these specialists can make a diagnosis; they know the possibilities for medical and ritual treatment. The prayers in the psalms come from their knowledge; indeed they are liturgical parts of worship which are to bring healing (similar rituals are known from the ancient Near East and many tribal societies), and they give us insight into the symptoms of suffering and their interpretation.

> 10. My heart throbs, my strength fails me; and the light of my eyes – it also has gone from me.
> 11. My friends and companions stand aloof from my plague, and my kinsmen stand far off.
> 13. Those who seek my life lay their snares, those who seek my hurt speak of ruin, and meditate treachery all the day long.
> 14. But I am like a deaf man, I do not hear, like a dumb man who does not open his mouth.
> 15. Yes, I am like a man who does not hear, and one who has nothing to say (Ps. 38.11–15).

The lament indicates stages in the suffering which to some degree correspond to the attitude of the deity. The physical collapse (v.11), already vividly described in vv.4, 6, 8, is the consequence of a divine 'curse', an evil reprimand. Other laments identify God's chastisement, blow, punishment, as the direct cause of this suffering. At all events God must be angry, and the reason for his anger can lie with the suppliant himself (vv.4.7). However, the punishment – no matter how deserved it may be – must not turn into anger (v.2), for then compassion could be excluded, and the measure of the punishment be exceeded (cf. Prov. 19.18). His closest kinsfolk stand round the sufferer; their solidarity is very important (cf. Ps. 35.11–15; 41.6–11). They have become sceptical: perhaps God's anger against the suppliant can no longer be turned away? Has the guardian deity already irrevocably doomed him to corruption? If that is the case, then everyone is exposed to the danger (v.12). The point is even reached when those closest of all to the sick person give up, in order to save their own skins (Ps. 41.10). What is the reaction of those more remote from the suppliant, those with whom he did not formerly get on? They openly and brutally urge the destruction of the one who is doomed to death (v.13). They quickly come up with the claim that God has clearly rejected this fellow (Ps. 22.8f.; 31.14; 55.34; 59.2–5; 69.5; 70.3f.; 71.10f.; 109.2–5; 143.3, etc.). The mass of references to enemies 'within', people who live in the same community or share the same faith and yet wish ill to the sufferer, is terrifying. It is a sign of the state of psycho-social tension in which the psalms of lamentation were uttered.[7] Theologically, however, the enemies stand for the turning away of God. It is not fortuitous that a mocking remark is put on their lips: 'He committed his cause to Yahweh. Let him rescue him, if he delights in him' (Ps. 22.9), along with the decisive, deadly question, 'Where is your God?' (Ps. 42.4). It casts the one who is threatened into the abyss. The sufferer has already internalized all the objections to him. He has already half given himself over to the ambivalence of hope and despair (vv.14f.). He no longer has any counter-arguments. He believes in his guilt (vv.18f.); he has noted God's anger and turning away and can only ask against all reason for help (vv.16f., 22f.). Despair lowers in the darkest tones, takes up the godforsakenness (Ps.22.2: 'My God, my God, why have your forsaken me') and extends to the sharpest accusations against the one who should really be a protector and benefactor (Ps. 88.7–19), in extreme cases even cursing the suppliant's own life (Jer. 20.14–18; Job 3.2–26).

So the question of God arises in the human environment[8] and on the basis of the personal fortunes of one who has been pursued by unhappiness. It is sparked off by symptoms of sickness, misery and persecution. Those who want to distance themselves from this lapse into death express the issue clearly. Where is the power that keeps you alive? Your God has failed, and now you've lost your chance. This is no metaphysical matter. God is experienced through this-worldly problems. The victims suffer the absence of God to a greater degree than they can say. Job, the great protester – but a literary figure, not a suppliant in a liturgical service – can accuse God of arbitrariness and misconduct (cf. Job. 19.6–22). The suppliant keeps silent and hopes.

The starting point for the ancient Israelite suppliant is the wider family which supports him. But that begins to fall victim to the disaster. Following its urge for survival, it withdraws its solidarity from the one who seeks it. One might almost call the godforsaken person in an industrial society fortunate. Such people do not need the social net of the family, and hardly know it from their everyday experience. Left to themselves – as latch-key children, engaged in single combat in school and profession, or as old people living in garrets – such people know what it means to be delivered over to death and marginalization. Indeed, they are there: the cries of the prisoners and the tortured, for mother and children, for wife or husband, brothers and sisters and relatives. But today the question of God seems less affected by the collapse of inter-personal solidarity in the most intimate circle. Rather, it is the triumph of injustice which agonizingly puts God's power in question. Where the family is no longer the sole support, its collapse is no longer experienced as the fundamental shattering of life. By contrast, the collapse of the legal order and of economic existence, chronic illnesses and permanent pain, can still provoke the question of God, even among people who do not regard themselves as being very religious. 'How can God do this to me?' 'If there is a just God, then he must help me.'

At that time, as today, the experience of the remoteness of God oscillated between desperation and hope. There was some prayer and some cursing. And when strength disappears and there is increasingly clearly no way out, apathetic endurance remains as the last resistance against the meaninglessness of suffering and dying. 'Hope dies last!'[9] The Psalmists live by the remnants of the primal trust which counts on the solidarity of the guardian deity. This solidarity is part of the family circle, is its invisible head. So it must be taken at its word and honoured, and called on for the help that is owed (cf. Ps. 38.21f.: 'Do not forsake me, Yahweh my God, be not far from me. Make haste to help me, O God of my salvation'). The petition can be like a hymn praising the qualities of God as protector and saviour (cf. Ps. 3.4; 13.6; 27.1; 28.1; 71.1–3, etc.). The frequent address to God as 'my God', 'my fortress', 'my deliverer' indicates the close personal tie to the deity. It is indeed shaken by the experience of the remoteness of God, but it is not done away with by either side. Given their secularized environment, it is far more difficult for modern men and women to activate so close a personal tie to God. Nevertheless, they think, pray and lament in the old patterns.

And what is their hope? Like the psalmists of old, they long for just one thing: a break-through to life. Having escaped once again, we would like a new chance just short of the abyss. In the Psalms that is an occasion for making vows (cf. Ps. 35.18; 42.12). The close and familiar deity can be offered something for deliverance (cf. Gen. 28.20f.). But the support expected from God does not consist in the bringing in of the eternal kingdom but in the restoration of normal life. Disruptions and hurts must cease. So health and a good outcome are the aim, and often enough the enemies will be punished or destroyed as those who had a share in the cause of the suffering (cf. Ps. 31.18f.; 35.26f.; 55.10–16; 109.6–20). Again we come up against the social problem of the absence of God. However much for Christ's sake we may eliminate any thought of vengeance from our prayers uttered in distress, the removal of social evils which cause the suffering of the many is an unconditional presupposition for the rehabilitation of the hungry. Poverty, the 'new' poverty, is a scourge of our time. The number of those who have been forced to the margin is growing rapidly, not only in the Third World countries, but also in industrial countries, in the midst of the greatest prosperity of all time. The unjust distribution of goods on this rich earth is itself a reason for noting God's impotence – not to mention the mechanisms of exploitation which the followers of the Christian God have invented in the course of history.

The godforsakenness seems to weigh that much more heavily when it affects a community, a people, a nation. The individual may give up after a while, because his strength may no longer be sufficient for the quest. 'Deny God and die!' (Job 2.9). Job is an exception. Most of the godforsaken go under, often no longer capable of lamenting. In the Psalms there are collective laments as well as individual laments. They express the desperation in dramatic words. A battle has been lost. God has shown himself incapable of helping his people or unwilling to help them. The accusation sounds very harsh.

> You have made us like sheep for the slaughter,
> and have scattered us among the nations.
> You have sold your people for a trifle,
> demanding no high price for them.
> You have made us the taunt of our neighbours,
> the derision and scorn of those about us.
> You have made us a byword among the nations,
> a laughingstock among the peoples (Ps. 44.11–14).

The petition is meant to compel God to show solidarity with his people once again. It harasses the absent God:

Rouse yourself! Why are you asleep, O Lord?
Awake! Do not cast us off for ever,
why do you hide your face?
Why do you forget our affliction and oppression?
For our soul is bowed down to the dust;
our body cleaves to the ground.
Rise up, come to our help!
Deliver us for the sake of your steadfast love! (Ps. 44.24–27).

The desperation becomes immeasurable when God's dwelling place, the sanctuary, is defiled by enemies (Ps. 74; cf. I Sam. 4f.) or when the holy city, Jerusalem, falls victim to war (Lam. 1; 2; 4; 5). Or the dynasty which supports the state falls, is wiped out, and the divine promises publicly given to it are shown to be of no account (Ps. 89). Are not such catastrophes clear evidence that God is impotent or uninterested – or even dead? And the godforsakenness which shows itself in defeats at the hands of enemies bears abundantly within itself the sting of the mockery of enemies (the theme is far less prominent in 'natural' calamities like drought and famine, plagues of locusts and earthquakes, cf. Jer. 14; Joel 1f.). But the enemies represent another deity, who has become stronger. They love to express their mockery in the cynical question, 'Where is your God?' (Ps. 79.10; 115.2; also Joel 2.17! cf. the vivid description of the blasphemous talk in II Kings 18.33–35). The taunts and mockery of the vanquished enemy were often ritualized in ancient societies: triumphal marches and victory parades are a survival of such demonstrations of humiliation. Many Old Testament texts speak of the mockery of the enemy and the shame suffered as a result. (cf. Ps. 14.14f.; 79.12; 80.7; 89.42).[10]

It emerges that even in wider societies conclusions are drawn from the state of the society as to God's absence. The lack of God's support in the face of hostile powers, possibly also in the face of natural threats, raises the question: Where is God? Has he turned away in wrath? Or is he asleep?

In our Western tradition since Constantine the Great the presence of God has been interwoven above all with the rule of the state. Until modern times the princes, kings and emperors who ruled 'by the grace of God' were the basic foundation of the social order. The nation states of the nineteenth century – including the democratic and later the secularized states – entered into this heritage. So it is that down to the present day the question of God plays an essential role at the national level which is not always clearly recognized. How does a people feel in times of national depression? Why do self-reproach, inferiority complexes, the feeling of forsakenness and victimization so easily turn into fanatical, nationalistic aggression? Are not mechanisms at work here which can only be explained by the desperate and continually frustrated search for the Absolute, for God? What happens in populations the majority of which belong to what Frantz Fanon called the 'wretched of the earth'? For decades they have experienced a steady deterioration in the economic situation and an ongoing lack of even the most basic human rights. How often in the past have people groaned in the endless slum settlements of the Third World (and sometimes even in the rich industrial world!) that starvation wages are no longer enough to live on! There have been short-term improvements and a long-term decline into an increasingly deep and unspeakably humiliating poverty. Can trust in God survive in such circumstances? It is a miracle that there are still communities of believers in the shanty-towns of Latin America. But for how long will the absence of God be tolerated? Atahualpa Yupangi (cf. above) thinks less than a generation.

The various conflicts of groups, classes and nations explode into bloody battles. Where is God in human wars? Apparently every armed struggle needs the support of God. Inhibitions about killing must be suppressed.[11] The name of the God who is the patron of the war does not matter. It must simply be seen as the supreme goal. All wars take place in the name of a God. Perhaps the situation of war in modern times is the last place where there is no problem in rapidly setting rationality aside, and the God who has long been said to be dead is again enthroned overnight.

But must we not distinguish between just wars and unjust wars, between exploitation by force and militant love? Indeed the distinction is necessary: the sober passion for justice and human dignity in many liberation movements is something fundamentally different from the blood-lust of monstrous bands of killers. With whom could God really be? May we make this question a test-case for the existence of God in our world?

The question of God which is derived from experience but is worked through intellectually is not alien to the Old Testament. It may have the upper hand in our time, and in the prosperous levels of society where people need not be concerned for their very existence. Science, technology and dissociation from 'primitive' pictures of the world guarantee it a high status. But antiquity knows similar reflections, and they are also expressed in the Psalms. The suppliant himself concedes that he has been drawn into intellectual doubt, like Job and Koheleth:

> But as for me, my feet had almost stumbled,
> my steps had well nigh slipped.
> For I was envious of the arrogant,
> when I saw the prosperity of the wicked (Ps. 73.2f.)

However, the Psalms often depict the type of the man of violence who has forgotten God, who stands over against God. They clearly indicate what a great impression these godless people make. The scornful confession 'There is no God' or – in complete indifference – 'I'm not bothered' causes serious inner conflicts among believers. This goes uncontradicted in practice. The suppliants in the Psalms suffer directly from the cynical claims of their tormentors. At the same time they are fascinated with the autonomy of these people, who have apparently cut out God's power.

> In the pride of his countenance the wicked does not seek God;
> all his thoughts are, 'There is no God.'
> His ways prosper at all times;
> your judgments are a matter of indifference to him.
> As for all his foes, he puffs at them.
> He thinks in his heart, 'I shall not be moved;
> throughout all generations I shall not meet adversity.
> His mouth is filled with cursing and deceit and oppression;
> under his tongue are mischief and iniquity.
> He sits in ambush in the villages;
> in hiding places he murders the innocent.
> His eyes stealthily watch for the hapless,
> he lurks in secret like a lion in his covert;
> he lurks that he may seize the poor;
> he seizes the poor when he draws him into his net.
> The hapless is crushed down, sinks down and falls by his might.
> He thinks in his heart, 'God has forgotten,
> he has hidden his face, he will never see it' (Ps. 10.4–11).

The attitude in the double Psalm 14/53 is quite similar. However, here the Psalmist reflects more on the enemies from outside who put on godless airs. Still, the problem is the same: God is no longer there, and the others claim at least with the semblance of justice and truth that for practical purposes he can be excluded. The suppliant himself becomes doubtful when confronted with this assertive atheism.

3. Where is our God now?

Today, are we more 'godforsaken' than earlier epochs? Hardly. However, the absence, inactivity and silence of God do of course oppress us, in the structures of society and thought which now prevail, as they did not in the biblical period or in the Middle Ages. The industrial revolution, the Enlightenment or post-modernity have come upon us like an avalanche, and they bear within themselves the deposits of earlier periods. Our age is surely characterized by the boundless individualism which is proclaimed on all sides, and the gnawing doubt that can rob the atomized masses of the right seedbed for a fulfilled life. Autonomous man easily freezes in his solitude. He is prone to being manipulated. To a terrifying degree he falls beneath the wheels of a society orientated on success. The phenomena of disintegration are multiplying in the economic gap between North and South. Majorities are excluded from an existence which is worth living. Minorities rule, exploit and appeal to divine right.

The call for the absent God who wills to be there for every creature can still be heard clearly. It is also taken up here and there and translated into saving reality. Wherever 'one of the least of these' (cf. Matt. 25.40) experiences the solidarity of others, God shows his presence. But we should not give way to any illusions. Even if quantifying thought is hardly in place in any 'proof of God', many, very many, of 'the least of these brothers' are dying 'in the fields, without prayer or confession' (cf. above). It is not a matter of their number; anyone who perishes in this way is a proof against God. Anyone who is forsaken is an accusation; any of them indicates that those around him or her who talk of God do not want to do anything for the survival of God in this world. For God does not die from intellectual erosion but from the twisting of righteousness and love.

The same can be said of the manifold human societies. Every conceivable formation, from the perspectives of class, race, gender, faith, language, culture, nationality or race, is an artificial construction, as it were a corset for life. Wherever these groups pursue their interests in a self-centred way by exercising power – and unfortunately that is the rule – and claim religious privileges in doing so, other groups are forced to the margin, disadvantaged, deprived of their rights and no longer have any possibilities in life. Blacks, foreigners, handicapped, women, old people, children, in prosperous societies are discriminated against by the ruling groups. According to the biblical understanding, such devaluation of the socially weaker is directed against the God who takes the side of the least ones. Discrimination kills God. That can be demonstrated from the biblical tradition. If only one God is the creator and sustainer of all human beings, then every creature is his child. But according to our ethical standards there cannot be any legal distinctions between the children of a couple. Anyone who in the name of his God encourages the power-struggle among groups on this earth betrays the one God who wills to be mother and father of all.

Last of all we must also reflect theologically in the narrower sense on the crying of the sufferers and the demands for the social equality of all people. Where do we find the God who can be so present in our contemporary situation that the desperate cries of humankind are answered and the spreading apathy is transformed into life? Where is the God of Jesus Christ, who heals individuals and groups by his love? He does not sit on thrones nor does he dwell in cathedrals. He is also among injured men and women and in his maltreated creation. He is the victim of blasphemous power.

> This swollen face, dirty and covered in sweat,
> marked by falls or blows,
> is the face
> of a drinker, a beggar,
> or are we even standing on the mount of Calvary
> and looking into the holy countenance of the Son of God?[12]

Translated by John Bowden

Notes

1. Cf. Horst Eberhard Richter, *Der Gotteskomplex*, Reinbek 1979.
2. Atahaulpa Yupangi, in *Cantare*, ed. Carlos Rincon and Gerda Schattenberg-Rincon, Dortmund 1980, 21f.
3. In *Hiob 1943*, ed. Karin Wolff, Neukirchen-Vluyn 1983, 153f. Original Polish: Izabela Gelbard, *Piesni zalobne getta*, Warsaw 1946.
4. Ibid., 155.
5. Stephen W. Hawking, *A Brief History of Time*, London and New York 1987.
6. Jacques Monod, *Chance and Necessity*, London and New York 1970.
7. Cf. Othmar Keel, *Feinde und Gottesleugner*, Stuttgart 1969.
8. Cf. Santos Benetti, *Salmos al derecho y al reves*, Marid 1977; id., *Salmos para viver y morir – Ensayo sobre la paradoja humana*, Madrid 1978.
9. Joao Cabral de Melo Neto, *Tod und Leben des Severino*, St Gallen and Wuppertal 1985.
10. Cf. M. A. Klopfenstein, *Scham und Schande nach dem Alten Testament*, Zurich 1972.
11. René Girard, *La violence et le sacré*, Paris 1972.
12. Helder Camara, *Mille raisons pour vivre*, Paris 1980.

Sickness and the Silence of God

Gregory Baum

The things that happen to us sometimes force upon us theological reflection. Certain events are able to challenge our very faith.

What is the meaning and message of God when you are very ill? This was the troubling question I had to wrestle with when I fell ill in March of this year (1990), suffering from a viral infection in the inner ears. For about eight weeks I was completely demobilized. I laid in bed in a dark room, unable to read or watch television. During these weeks of total silence my condition did not improve. I was in pain: I felt as if my head and parts of my body were caught in a cage that did not fit. Fortunately I had a wife who looked after me with great care. And I was grateful to the graduate students who helped her do the shopping.

Lying in bed I had time to think. I actually divided my days into periods, each assigned to a different topic for prayer and reflection. One period was for day-dreaming. Yet most of the time I dealt with the troubling question: Was this illness God's will? What if I never regain my health? Would this be God's will too?

An important current of Catholic spirituality greatly emphasizes surrender to God. Because God is the heavenly Father who has revealed his love in Jesus Christ, we are summoned to trust God, detach ourselves from our own plans, abandon all fear, and deliver ourselves to the divine will. If we fall ill, if we suffer, if we lose the people we love, we should remember the suffering of Jesus, join our own suffering to his, and trustingly surrender ourselves to the gracious will of God. This is what Jesus did in the garden: not my will, but thy will be done.

In my illness I found this unconditional surrender very difficult.

Over the years I had been affected by the religious literature, produced by Jews and by Christians, dealing with the God-question after the Holocaust and the other organized massive, death-dealing cruelty of the twentieth century. Come to think of it, I actually have made a modest contribution to this literature. Is this enormous human suffering, which still continues, the will of a loving God? According to traditional theology, Jewish and Christian, God does not will evil directly: still, God permits it to happen. No event takes place, it is argued, without the permission of the Omnipotent. Is this answer still acceptable? Did God give permission for Auschwitz and Hiroshima? Does God give permission for cancer and other illnesses?

The question of God and evil is an ancient one. It greatly troubled the biblical authors. Yet in the twentieth century, because of the massive destructions of human beings, this question has been posed with a new urgency. According to a Jewish religious thinker, one consequence of the Holocaust has been 'the end of untroubled theism'. From now on, belief in God troubles us profoundly. The more we believe that God is love, the more difficult we find it to believe in God.

Influenced by this religious reflection, I found it impossible to accept my illness as God's will. Can one trust God, I asked myself, can one surrender oneself to God, if this divinity has allowed 'the new darkness' of the twentieth century?

And yet when you are ill and disabled, you do not want to be at odds with your sickness. If a patient is angry at his illness, he becomes irritable and restless. What I desired was above all to be calm, to accept my condition, to have patience. Such an acceptance is the spiritual condition for physical healing. I wanted to be at peace.

While I could not utter prayers of surrender, I had no trouble in praying for health, spiritual and physical. I became profoundly attached to Jesus, the healer, *Christus medicus*, as the ancients called it. Jesus, the healer of body and soul. I came to think of God as rescuer and restorer of life. This appealed to me enormously. Even if I should never fully recover, my hope was that God would strengthen my soul so that I could live peacefully in the handicapped situation.

I then dropped the question whether my illness was God's will. God's will, I felt, was my healing – 'spiritually understood'. God does not will sickness: on the contrary, God is the principle of life, the source of the spiritual and physical energies that enable people to transcend their wounded condition and live richly and deeply. In this context I found it easy to surrender myself to God's will, for this will was my health and my rescue – 'spiritually understood'.

When I prayed for health and rescue, I always added 'spiritually understood' so as to be open to the possibility of lasting mental or bodily damage where health and rescue means peace of mind in the situation of handicap.

Yet I cannot deny that during the first two weeks when I was in constant misery, I strongly felt that if this condition were to be chronic, the gracious God, life-giver and rescuer, would allow me to put an end to my life. This went against the teaching of the church. Still, in my misery I received great consolation from the idea that God had left me this last door to freedom.

What follows for me from these reflections is that it is unhelpful to think of God as heavenly emperor ruling the world from above and giving permission for suffering and evil. God's omnipotence must be understood differently. Omnipotence refers rather to God's limitless power to create, to redeem, to heal, to reconcile and restore. God here grounds and supports all of life and all of being.

This idea is not foreign to the classical theological tradition. While I was sick I was amazed how important the old Thomistic teaching of God as Pure Act and Unmoved Mover became to me. Since this teaching is often presented in an unfavourable light, let me explain how I read it and what it meant to me.

In the Aristotelian-Thomistic perspective, all beings are composed of two principles, 'act' and 'potency'. Act here refers to the form or essence of a being. Act is the principle of action, realization and fulfilment. Potency, on the other hand, refers to the as yet unrealized possibilities of a being. All beings are combinations of act and potency. While this 'hylomorphic' cosmological theory is no longer accepted by contemporary thinkers, it still generates interesting images of the Divine.

How, according to this philosophy, can one explain the movement from potency to act? How does the acorn become an oak? How do beings grow, develop, become perfected, and realize their potentiality? Above all how do humans actualize their powers? According to this philosophy, beings are not self-moving. Whatever is moved is moved by another. The passage from potency to act in any being depends therefore on the power extended to it from another being that is richer in actuality. But one cannot account for life, growth, development and realization of all beings without affirming the existence of One, an infinite One, who is totally act and who initiates the movement from potency to act in all beings.

Here we have then the two technical terms, God as Pure Act and Unmoved Mover. What do these terms mean? If they are not clarified with the help of the hylomorphic theory, they sound abstract and heartless, as if the divinity, perfect in heavenly splendour, were unmoved by the fate of men and women. When the Scholastics called God Pure Act, they suggested that God was not a being, that God differed from all beings inasmuch as God was fully realized and activated, free of all potency. For example, God was fully loving: God's love could not increase, because God was love. And secondly – this is important in our context – God was related to men and women not so much as heavenly ruler but as the creative, life-giving, actualizing presence at the core of their being. God was mover: which was to say God was the gracious, vivifying presence in their lives that enabled them to actualize their potency – to grow, develop, become wise and loving. God was mover, prompting men and women to enter more fully into their humanity. Today we hold that God is mover, empowering people in their struggle for dignity and justice.

Reflecting on God as Pure Act and Unmoved Mover during my illness, I had the strong realization that people who yearn and struggle for their physical and spiritual health, do so because they are so moved by God: their entry into actualization is prompted by the loving God who is totally Act. In moving people to enter into their destiny, God – the Scholastics insisted – is 'unmoved', i.e. not in need of a prompter or enabler. God's self-communication in creation, redemption and providence takes place out of the infinite resources of God's own actuality.

If this theology is valid, then the surrender to God in prayer is at the same time an affirmation of all the human struggles for health and well-being, spritually understood, struggles – as we have seen – in which God is graciously present to men and women. These struggles include more especially the wrestling of the exploited and oppressed for the conditions of life in keeping with their dignity. If God is Pure Act, then turning to God does not separate us from our own depth or from other people. Here the prayer of surrender is no longer frightening since it is a surrender to life and rescue, to the life and rescue of all.

I cannot deny that this thought was consoling to me in my illness. It made the prayer of surrender possible and gave it political meaning.

(This is a short sermon I gave in the chapel of McGill University after recovering from a severe illness.)

The Presence and Revelation of God in the World of the Oppressed

Pablo Richard

Nothing is more disturbing than the presence of God in the world of the oppressed and the absence of God in the world of the oppressors. Today a new international order is being forced upon the world in which the rich get richer and the poor get poorer. A free-market economy is being imposed upon us as the only possibility, in which the guests at the liberal banquet celebrate the end of history and the end of utopias. The excluded (the great majority of the human race) are condemned as guilty victims, whose sacrifice is inevitable and ultimately pleasing to Moloch or Mammon, the god of history. This article seeks to show how the logic of the God of life destroys this whole idolatrous order and banquet of the oppressors. It also sets out to show the wealth and spiritual power of those who are excluded and humiliated by the new modern Western liberal euphoria. The world of the oppressed is poor in power, money, technology and arms, but rich in humanity and spirituality.

1. The presence of God and how to distinguish it from idolatry

In the world of the oppressed the quest for God is in conflict not with modern atheism, but with oppressive idolatry. The atheism which exists in the world of the oppressed is not the enlightened atheism of modern people, but the critical atheism of the revolutionaries and prophets. The world of the excluded is pre-modern or anti-modern, and in it the types of atheism characteristic of the modern era have no importance. What does have a certain influence is critical atheism, but this is not directed against the poor and believing people, but against the idolatrous system of the oppressors. This atheism is a reaction against the manipulation or perversion of the name of God or against the routine, easy faith of the dominant world which does not respect the experience of the transcendent and the absolute in the world of the poor. Often there is an alliance between the critical atheists and the prophetic believers against the idolatry of the oppressive world. The danger to faith therefore does not come from the atheist revolutionaries, but from the idolatrous oppressors.

The fundamental theological task in the world of the oppressed is not so much to prove the existence of God, but to distinguish the true God from the false idols. The problem is not how we can know if God exists, but to show which God we believe in. The theological battle is not against the atheists to prove the existence of God, but against the idolaters, to show where God is, what God is like, who God is with, who God is against, what God's plan is, and how God makes himself present and reveals himself in history. The fundamental problem is not the existence of God, but his presence. Proving the existence of God is an abstract and fairly easy task of a philosophical kind; what is much more difficult and important is to show the privileged presence of God in the world of the oppressed and their struggles for liberation. From an apologetic theology concerned with the proofs of the existence of God we are moving to a spiritual theology which is about discerning the presence of God in our history. This theology and this discernment are not carried out in opposition to prophetic or critical atheism, but in opposition to the dominant idolatry.

2. The God of Life and the idols of death

Distinguishing the true God from false idols is a task of concern not just to theologians, but to the whole people of God. Every oppressed believer feels the need to stress the difference between the God in which they believe and the dominant idolatry. Afro-American theology says, 'God is black', to stress the difference from the dominant racist ideology. The theology of women's liberation also says 'God is she', to stress the difference from the dominant patriarchal ideology. In a similar way, in the theology of liberation we say 'God of the poor' or 'God of Life', to stress the difference from the idols of death. God certainly has no colour or sex or wealth, but what all these expressions are trying to affirm is the difference between the experience of God which the oppressed have and the idolatrous images of God cultivated by the dominant system. This task of distinguishing between the God of Life and the idols of death is thus not just a theological problem, but a problem of life and death for the poor and oppressed. The 'battle of the gods' is a spiritual warfare waged at the heart of history, in the minds of believers, in the church and in society.

3. Idolatries ancient and modern

In the Bible we find two basic forms of idolatry, idolatry by perversion and idolatry by substitution. The first takes place in direct relation to Yahweh, when the very name or image of God is manipulated or perverted. The second takes place when Yahweh is replaced by other gods or false gods. Exodus 32 is the most typical example of idolatrous perversion in the people's relationship with Yahweh. The most abundant texts, however, are those which battle against foreign gods or the false gods which replace Yahweh. This critique of idolatry is the fundamental thrust of the whole Bible. Typical texts of this critique are Jer. 10.1–6; Isa. 44.14–17; Ps. 115; Wisdom 13–15. The New Testament mainly criticizes the idolatry of money, of the law, of power and knowledge. In the book of Revelation the two great sins are murder and idolatry, the destruction of the human being and the perversion of the sense of God.

Nowadays idolatry is a growth industry. There is idolatry by perversion when the proper sense of God is lost, when God is manipulated, his image is deformed or his name is used in vain. The producers of this type of idolatry are those who call themselves Christians and are oppressors: the Christian *conquistadores*, colonialists and slave-owners in the Third World since the sixteenth century, Christian industrialists and bankers who oppress the people, racist and sexist Christians. There is also idolatry by substitution when the God of Life is replaced by oppressive false gods. This takes place when human beings make gods or absolutes out of the works of their hands, the god Money, the god Capital, the god Power, the god Technology, the god Institution, the god I. The idolatrous perversion of God and the creation of idols of death generates the 'spiritual power' of any system of domination; it is what gives it power and legitimacy to go on oppressing and dominating.

4. Idolatry as the root of social sin

In Latin America we talk a lot about social sin, and rightly, because this sin exists and its consequences are tragic. Social sin is not an anonymous, blind or inevitable force, but structures of sin created by human beings, for which they are responsible. But social sin is not the ultimate reality which oppresses us, nor the explanation for the situation of death we suffer. There is something behind social sin which gives it power and efficacy. A sinner cannot sin without limit, because every sinner has a bad conscience and dies in their sin and through their sin. In social sin, however, we find that there are no limits: the system oppresses and kills without limit and with a clear conscience. This oppression without limits and with a clear conscience is the result of idolatry, which is the transcendent spiritual force of death which gives life and a clear conscience to the sinner responsible for social sin. Idolatry comes into being when historical agents of oppression identify themselves with a transcendent, universal subject in the name of which they practise oppression. The oppressive system appropriates and identifies itself with a spiritual system of values in the name of which it practises oppression. This identification with a divine subject created by the same system is what allows the system to oppress without limits and with a clear conscience. This means that idolatry is not a harmless spiritual deviation, but what gives power and legitimacy to the oppressive system. Idolatry is highly criminal and dangerous. Idolatry is the supernatural power of death which is keeping social sin alive. St Paul expresses it very well: 'Our battle is not against human powers, but against the governments and authorities who direct this world *and its dark forces; we face the supernatural spirits and powers of evil*' (Eph. 6.12).

The dominant system produces not only material goods, but also idols and idolatry. The system has the capacity to produce spiritual and supernatural powers of death, to create a world which is transcendent, numinous, fantastic. When the dominant economic, political and cultural power succeeds in creating this spiritual dimension, power has more power. There is a multiplication of power. Idolatrized or spiritualized power is more powerful than simple material historical power. Idolatry is therefore a way of increasing power. By faith we know that this whole spirituality is false, an idolatrous human creation, but the dominant power, by generating this spiritual force, increases its power and this multiplied and increased power is real and tremendously effective. Idolatrous power is more effective than non-idolatrized power. As a result, idolatry is power, a power which produces more power and a production of power without limits; it projects itself without limit on to the absolute, the infinite, the spiritual, the supernatural, the transcendent. This whole production of power takes place in a false consciousness, but the power which is able to create this consciousness and impose it as the dominant consciousness really increases its power. Idolatry is false, but the production of power is not an illusion; it is real. Idolatrized power is more dangerous, and strikes harder and deeper than non-idolatrized power.

The dominant economic, political and cultural power creates idols, not only to increase its power, but also to exercise spiritual domination over people and society. An idolatrous society is not only a society which is dominated economically, politically and culturally; it is also a society dominated spiritually. Idolatry gives domination a spiritual, supernatural and transcendent depth. All this idolatrous power and domination is reinforced, multiplied and legitimized when it has churches, sects and spiritualist movements at its service. The idolatry becomes uncontainable, and penetrates the whole of society. The root of idolatry is in the dominant power, but this power can convert the whole culture and the dominant religion into mechanisms of spiritual domination. Because of this, idolatry is not only a theological deviation or a perversion of conscience, an inner, private, neutral phenomenon. On the contrary, idolatry is a dimension of the dominant power, a social phenomenon, highly dangerous, which affects society and individuals at their root and permeates them totally.

If idolatry is the spiritual force of the dominant economic, political and cultural power, if idolatry has both a social and an individual, a spiritual and a material dimension, the believer's battle against idolatry has to be equally radical, wide-ranging and deep-rooted. The battle against idolatry is not only a theological or personal battle, not only a spiritual problem or one for the individual conscience, but also a specific dimension of the historical practice of liberation. The believer in the true God faces the idols of the system and the idolatry of death in a total and all-absorbing battle, in all areas of social, personal, material and spiritual life. Because of this the theology of liberation insists that faith has to be lived and expressed within a practice of liberation. Faith is the authentically spiritual and transcendent dimension of the practice of liberation. Faith's spiritual warfare is experienced as a specific and deeply rooted dimension of the economic, political and cultural practice of liberation. When faith sets us free from idols and idolatry, this is not just a spiritual and personal liberation, but the inherent depth of a historical, social and political liberation.

5. The transcendent and liberating experience of God in history

There is only one history, and God is present, reveals himself and saves us within this one history. To have faith is to believe that God intervenes in history and that is why we confess him as the God of history. To have faith is to believe that in history there is always a transcendent presence of God and a word of God to surprise us. History is the basic mediation of encounter with God. All these statements make up the basic common tradition of any liberation theology.

A key concept for understanding history as the mediation of the presence, revelation and salvation of God is the concept of transcendence.

Etymologically, the word refers to something which is beyond a limit. What is beyond the limit is transcendent, and what is within the limit is immanent. It is therefore important to define what this limit is. There are two sorts of limit, different but related. The first is oppression. The person who is oppressed is limited by the structures of oppression, all sorts of structures: economic, political, cultural, ethnic, sexist, ideological and religious. If we take this first limit as our criterion, God is transcendent because he frees us from oppression. God breaks the chains, frees us from all the limits oppression imposes on us, and enables us to live in fullness beyond these limits. God is thus transcendent because he is a liberator and a liberator because he is transcendent. The liberating and transcendent God does not tolerate oppression and enables the oppressed to live beyond the limits imposed by oppression. That is why transcendence is so important for the poor, because the transcendent God is the God who liberates from all oppression.

The second limit is more universal and radical, death. Every creature experiences this limit. God is transcendent in this case because he surpasses this limit and guarantees life beyond death. Immanent life is life which ends with death, and transcendent life is that which overcomes death once and for all. That is what we call eternal life, that is, a life which does not die. God is transcendent because he is the God who liberates from oppression and also because he is the God who liberates from death. The transcendent God is the God of Life, because he guarantees a fully liberated life, a life without oppression and without death.

This life which is liberated (without oppression) and eternal (without death) is life in history. God does not transcend history, but transcends oppression and death within our history, which also means that all history is transformed by the presence of God. God frees us from oppression and death in our history. Very often we think of transcendence as what is beyond the visible realm, beyond the material realm, beyond history. The transcendent, on this view, is the invisible, the non-material, the a-historical or trans-historical. This is a false conception of transcendence, or at least is not the biblical, liberating concept of transcendence. In the Bible transcendence is abundant life, material, bodily, historical life, fully enjoyed beyond all oppression and beyond death. God is transcendent because he frees us, not from the body or from matter, but from oppression and death. Abundant life is bodily life which never dies. This presupposes faith in the resurrection, the transformation of our mortal bodies, the transfiguration of our matter, the glorification of our historical existence. Faith in the bodily and historical resurrection of the flesh has always been a

central element of the theology of liberation. This concept of transcendence as the overcoming of death is something exclusive to faith. It is
our faith in God as transcendent which allows us to hope for the
resurrection, the transformation of our mortal bodies into immortal life,
life which never dies. We insist that this abundant life takes place within
history, in an immortal, transfigured and glorified, but historical, form.
We do not know exactly what this abundant, immortal bodily life will be
like, but we hope for it as a new creation of the liberating and transcendent
God within our one history.

Biblical language is the most appropriate for enabling us to understand
this intra-historical transcendence, not because it reflects a specific culture,
but because it best expresses how the believing poor and oppressed
experience the transcendent God within history. Let us take, as an
example, two biblical texts in clear continuity with each other, Isaiah
65.17–25 and Revelation 21.1–22.5. Both texts combine cosmic language
with historical language. The cosmic language is not a-historical, but
designed solely to radicalize the prophet's historical experience. Here are
extracts from the two texts:

> *Isaiah 65*: For behold, I shall create new heavens and a new earth . . .
> For behold, I create Jerusalem a rejoicing and her people a joy. I will
> rejoice in Jerusalem and be glad in my people; no more shall be heard in
> it the sound of weeping and the cry of distress. No more shall there be in
> it an infant that lives but a few days, or an old man who does not fill out
> his days, for dying young will be dying at a hundred . . . They shall
> build houses and inhabit them; they shall plant vineyards and eat their
> fruit. They shall not build and another inhabit; they shall not plant and
> another eat . . . my chosen shall long enjoy the work of their hands . . .
> The wolf and the lamb will feed together.

In this text what is overcome is clearly oppression. The new creation of the
cosmos, the city and the people is the creation of a world without
oppression. God proclaims abundant life, where children do not die,
without exploitation, robbery, suffering or wars, but death continues to
exist. There is no longer early death, as a result of oppression, but in the
end there is death. Let us look now at the other text:

> *Revelation 21–22*: Then I saw a new heaven and a new earth . . . And I
> saw the holy city, the new Jerusalem . . . and death shall be no more,
> neither shall there be mourning nor crying nor pain any more, for the
> former things have passed away . . . The glory of God is the light [of the

city]. There are trees of life . . . They shall see his face . . . The Lord God will be their light, and they shall reign for ever and ever.

Now there is a clear overcoming even of death. Heaven and earth here represent the cosmos, and the city represents social organization. The cosmos and the city are new in so far as there is no longer death in them. It is a world transformed, lit by the glory of God, in which everyone will see God directly. There is a new creation, a new cosmos and a new social organization, and so history continues, but now without death and with a visible presence of the glory of God. The material and bodily continuity of history and the discontinuity of death are both essential elements in the text. Other biblical texts express this continuity of history and overcoming of death in the image of the new man and the new woman, the new creature, the spiritual body. Jesus' resurrection itself is the model of this transformation: the risen Jesus is the same Jesus, bodily present (he is not a ghost; he eats with his disciples), but at the same time there is a transformation, a glorification: they do not recognize him except through the word and the breaking of the bread.

6. The God of the Bible

The deep root of our theo-logy is the experience of God in the world of the poor. God makes himself present and reveals himself in history and life as the God who liberates the oppressed and as the God who guarantees life for all, especially for the poor. This experience of God has to be discerned and expressed. The Bible is the criterion or canon for the carrying out of this work of discernment. According to St Augustine, God wrote two books, the book of life and the Bible. In the history of the liberation both of the cosmos and of the human race, God communicated with us. However, because of sin, and above all because of idolatry, which has filled the world with so much 'religious verbiage', so much 'spirituality of death', so much 'theological ideology', a second book was necessary, to help us to read the first. This second book was the Bible. St Augustine says, 'The Bible, God's second book, was written to help us to decipher the world, to give us back the eyes of faith and contemplation, and to transform all things into a great revelation of God.' The Bible is thus the fundamental criterion we have for discerning the living word of God in our lives and our history. We say that God makes himself present and reveals himself in a special way in the world of the poor, and the Bible is the basic instrument for discerning that presence and that word and enabling us to articulate it, say it, communicate it, shout it out to the whole world.

It is classical teaching to distinguish three meanings in the Bible: the literal meaning, the historical meaning and the spiritual meaning. The literal meaning is the meaning the text has as a text, as an independent, organized literary structure. The historical meaning is the meaning the text acquires in the light of the history in which the text originated and in which the text became part of history. The spiritual meaning is the meaning the text receives when it is read to discern and communicate the word of God in our present situation. In other words, the Bible has meaning when we interpret the text in itself, when we interpret past history in which the text came into being, and when the text interprets our situation and transforms it into 'a great revelation of God'. We read the Bible, and the Bible itself reads our situation. When we discover the literal, historical and spiritual meanings of the Bible, the Bible is transformed into the mediation of the word of God in history. The Bible ceases to be a dead text and rises as a living mediation of the word of God. This discovery and resurrection of the Bible, through the recovery of its literal, historical and spiritual meanings, takes place with the help of biblical scholarship, in the life of the Christian community, itself inserted into the process of liberation of the people. Discovering the literal and historical meaning normally requires the help of biblical scholarship, but the discovering the spiritual meaning requires above all the Holy Spirit, whose action comes to life and takes effect in the faith of the ecclesial community inserted into history. The exegete essentially brings his or her scholarship, the community brings both its faith in the Spirit of truth and its human and political knowledge of the history of liberation of which it is a part. When the exegete shares the political and spiritual experience of the community, and when the community too has an understanding of biblical scholarship, the Bible multiplies even more its ability to mediate the word of God.

7. The God of the people of God

The fundamental mediation of the experience of God in the history of salvation has always been the people of God, and in first place the people of the poor and oppressed. As early as the exodus God appears as the one who sees the humiliation of his people and hears their cry. God makes an alliance with the people, and it is the people which liberates the promised land and takes possession of it. The people organizes itself at Shechem as a confederation of twelve tribes, and as a people recognizes God as king. It is the people which preserves the oral tradition, as the historical memory of the poor, out of which the Bible later emerges. When the beasts which oppress the people are destroyed, it is the people of the saints which receives power (Daniel 7). Jesus is born identified with his people, and when he begins his ministry organizes the community of the twelve apostles. Jesus sheds his blood as the blood of the New Covenant shed for the many. The Holy Spirit descends on the people of the New Covenant. At the end of the ages God renews his covenant with the whole human race, symbolized by the new Jerusalem: 'This is the dwelling-place of God with human beings; from this time on his dwelling-place shall be in their midst and they will be his people and he himself shall be God-with-them' (Rev. 21.3). Experience of God takes place essentially in the historical experience of being the people of God. Nothing is more opposed to God's teaching method than religious individualism or spiritualism. The experience of God is always a people's experience.

The ecclesial base community is the most immediate and tangible embodiment of the people of God in Latin America. The base community as such is the fundamental, most solid, explicit and popular mediator of the experience of God today in Latin America, especially among the poor and oppressed. When believers organize themselves into base communities, they begin to live, think, communicate and celebrate their experience of God in a radically different way. Only in a small community do people who for centuries have been excluded begin to take an active and creative part in the rebuilding of the church. The oppressed begin to create, from their historical experience and their own culture, a new spirituality, new symbols, new prayers, a new way of celebrating faith, of reading the Bible and reflecting on faith. If God makes himself present and reveals himself in a special way in the world of the poor and oppressed, the base communities are certainly the best illustration of this experience of God, insofar as they are the most direct ecclesial expression which originates in this world of the poor. All this becomes particularly visible and significant in the liberating spirituality of the base communities, and above all in the thousands and thousands of martyrs, who by laying down their lives, are revealing to us where and how God is present and active today in the history of Latin America.

The base communities are the germ of a new model of church which is coming into being today in Latin America, the church of the poor. This is not a new church, but a new way of thinking about and organizing the church. The fundamental mission of this new model of church is to make God credible in this world of the Third World, made up mainly of poor and oppressed. The base communities are the main force in the building of this new model of church, are its most visible part, but are by no means the whole of the church of the poor. The church of the poor also exists, though in a more diffuse and less visible form, in popular religion, popular spirituality, popular theology, especially in so far as this whole popular Christian world is touched or transformed by a liberating evangelization and gradually comes to identify with the most visible expression of the church of the poor. The church of the poor, on the other hand, is also not a sect, but represents the universal vocation of the whole church. The church of the poor is thus a universal church, through its deep roots in the world of the poor, who are the majority, but it is also a movement of conversion and renewal appealing to the whole church. This is the model of church which constitutes today in Latin America the fundamental mediation of the presence and revelation of God in the world of the oppressed.

In this whole new way of life in the church which is coming into being and growing in Latin America today, theology, the *magisterium* and the hierarchy all have the same role as that which tradition assigns them within the people of God. In so far as they express the sense of faith of the people of God, theology, the *magisterium* and the hierarchy, too, are real mediations of the experience of God. The theology of liberation, in dialogue and communion with the *magisterium* and the hierarchy, has played a notable role in mediating the experience of God in the world of the poor and oppressed. The most important feature of liberation theology is not its political dimension, but its experience of and talk about God in the world of the oppressed. This theology is not feared because it speaks about liberation, but because it speaks about God from the point of view of the poor and oppressed. What brought liberation theology into being is the experience of the absence of God in the idolatrous world of the oppressors, and the experience of the presence and special revelation of God in the world of the oppressed. The church of the poor is a church where people talk about the code of life, but above all it is a church in which the God of the poor himself can speak and make himself known to the whole of church and society. Very often the traditional church and traditional theology talk a lot about God, but God himself cannot speak in them. The church and theology must break with the idolatry of the dominant system if they are to learn to discern the disturbing presence of God in the world of the oppressed.

Translated by Francis McDonagh

Guilty and Without Access to God

Andrés Tornos

The distress of not finding a God to turn to is one felt particularly by those in great suffering. Does this distress have specific features today in those with a strong sense of the burden of guilt? That is the subject of this article.

1. Guilt today

At first sight it would seem that the distress of not finding a God to turn to in the humiliation of guilt would be a problem affecting very few people in our time. It is usually said that these days the sense of sin has become almost non-existent.

We know, however, that a sense of sin and guilt or a sense of guilt are not the same thing. A sense of sin is a recognition that we have done something which offends God. A sense of guilt, on the other hand, can affect anyone who feels that they have fallen from their own standard – whether sin is involved or not. For example, some people feel guilty because they live in comfort while many people are in need. Others, perhaps, feel guilty for not having brought up their children well or for having made serious professional mistakes (e.g. a doctor whose patient has died when he should have been able to save him). And in general we feel guilty when we do not meet deep, elemental expectations we have of ourselves.

Psychoanalysts have their own particular interpretation of these experiences of guilt, which are always uncomfortable and unpleasant and frequently cause us states of discomfort which create stress or atypical behaviour, and can turn into a secret inner torment or actual diseases. For the psychoanalysts the problem is always the secret experience of having failed our father (or mother!), those who in this life laid down for us both rules of behaviour and a space outside which we could not find either love or respect.

What is certain is that we experience a disagreeable emotional sensation when we feel that we are not being what we basically ought to be, but on the contrary are acting in a way which makes no sense for our personality. This produces the sensation of guilt. In such cases we can resort to very different strategies to relieve our distress, but this will have affected us like a secret sorrow, and almost never passes without leaving us emotionally wounded and slightly changed in attitude.

2. Special characteristics of guilt in contemporary societies

In the previous section I tried to describe the feeling of guilt which may be experienced today, but only in its most general outlines, those which make it like what might be experienced in any period. Nonetheless our inner feelings are always modified by cultural and social circumstances. It is therefore necessary, if we are considering the distress which may be caused by a feeling of guilt in our societies, where God is silent or absent, to go into more detail about some of the factors involved in feelings of guilt today. My reflections, of course, not being based on empirical studies, will be in the nature of suggestions and conjectures rather than firm pronouncements.

I have already referred indirectly to a first characteristic, the dissociation between a feeling of guilt and a sense of sin. This can have different effects on our feelings of guilt: on the one hand we may experience non-sinful failures for which we may feel guilty as less ours, and as a result, since we do not experience them as the effect of evil choices arising out of our free and responsible will, they do not become such a burden for us as things we have deliberately done and affirmed. On the other hand, we may perhaps experience them as more ours, because we feel alone with them, without institutions or myths which, in some cases, could relieve us of the inevitable burden of having failed.

Another characteristic which might affect our present-day attitudes and make us sorry for 'failures' is the large number and variety of investigators searching for guilty parties, mistakes or failings, who surround us on all sides today invested with a strange form of authority. This derives from the role which the communications media have come to play in present-day culture and attitudes. Before the media made themselves omnipresent in the social atmosphere, we bore the burden of our faults in the intimate forum of our own consciences and also in the sight of a small number of friends, and it was they who confronted us with society's demands. The voice which uttered the criticisms of our conduct of course spoke from within, as now, but it was echoed from without by only a few people, either by their words or by their mere presence. Sometimes the reverse happened, and the behaviour of the words of a small number of people was a reproach which was on occasion echoed by the consciences of those at fault. The authority of the outside critical voices, which were usually religious or from within the family, and very rarely from society as such, was either an authority with which negotiations were possible, and from which we could expect understanding, or one from which we could escape, at all events 'of limited jurisdiction'.

But now all this has changed. The media now provide the voices which echo our consciences; the media produce the thousands of echoes of our secret shames. Voices past counting indeed, given the prestigious dedication of moralizing cultivated by politicians and many journalists, though their moralities are different. But in the presence of so many voices listing evils which we cannot help finding in ourselves, to whom can we explain ourselves? Who will listen to us? What conversion rites or attempts at change will give us ourselves back the sense that we have begun to rebuild our social dignity?

A third feature of the sense of guilt in today's world is that it has no face, shape or name. In traditional culture things were different, if only because guilt and remorse for sin tended to be identified, so that when people felt guilty they felt able to recognize in their distress the features of that familiar feeling everyone called remorse. On that basis they either acknowledged themselves as sinners or acquitted themselves of any fault, but at any rate they knew what to do.

Today it's not like that. Even those who interpret their own feelings in the light of psychology are defenceless against the discomfort of guilt, except for a very few specialists. They find it difficult to unravel the damage to their ideal of the self which may underlie what they feel, or their anxieties about their relationship with society, or half-buried fantasies in which they are cheating people who have been very important in their lives. This difficulty completely blurs the outline of what they are feeling. Its aftertaste waylays them like a vague obstacle which it is impossible to identify, or like an enemy in disguise whose future movements are impossible to predict. In psychoanalytic jargon we would say that the truth of guilt remains unconscious today for the vast majority of those who experience it, and only surfaces in irritating episodes of being out of sorts with oneself and with one's social world.

From my own point of view I seem to notice this more clearly in the younger generations, in whom I have found, both in men and women, frequent discrepancies between the ideal of the self and actual everyday performance, between close emotional loyalties and practical behaviour connected with them, and at the same time an unspoken disappointment about this, although people offer all sorts of rationalizations and justifications for it. But perhaps I see this more clearly in the young because I am no longer young.

In short, I think that guilt today is experienced in a different way from previous periods, for example, in Freud's day. This is due in part to the dissociation between the feeling of guilt and the sense of sin, the ubiquitousness of moralizing authorities (with various sorts of morality) in the media and the loss of clear outlines of the territory we imagine ourselves to inhabit when we feel guilty.

3. Specific instances

Before continuing, I am going to illustrate my remarks with some specific cases, since it is obvious that looking at these will produce more clarity than keeping to general considerations.

The examples, of course, will be cases of guilt which we could call 'severe'. These are the ones we are concerned with, after all, since feeling guilty is something very common, and yet distress is not that common as a result of guilt, with or without an experience of the absence of God.

I am going to take four cases which may give rise to 'severe' experiences of guilt: that of parents who feel they have failed because of the life-style adopted by their children; that of those who in their youth joined generous political groups and subsequently have felt brutally disappointed by them; that of people trapped in drug addiction; and that of emigrants whose hopes for their families have not been fulfilled.

I myself have found severe feelings of guilt in people affected by such situations, feelings which left them feeling really unfortunate or distressed. At the same time these cases all shared the features which I previously defined as characteristic of the present way of experiencing guilt: at the beginning the people affected made no connection between the shame and inner distress they felt and any real or imaginary sense of sin, and felt that they were left alone to carry a terrible fate which befell them without any reason.

Again, in all the cases they treated various reports and arguments on television and in the press as directed personally at them. This happened in the first case with features on the lack of communication supposedly so common between parents and children and the negative effects this was said to produce, features on the behavioural problems allegedly produced when parents tried to solve domestic problems by giving their children lavish presents, money and so on.

In the case of individuals disappointed with their radical political choices, the guilt felt was more ambivalent. They became upset both when the media criticized the abandonment by the former idealists of their moral aims and when they criticized the former young radicals for naivety and lack of realism. They felt both types of interpretation to be allusions to their case.

The case of drug addiction I am thinking of was of an alcoholic. He was very upset about his addiction, as is not uncommon, and all the time he kept reinforcing his feelings of anger with what he read in the press about all sorts of addiction.

The same happened with a Latin American immigrant in the United States, who had left his children behind in their country of origin in the certainty that by emigrating he could prepare a better future for them. The strange thing is that in this case he accepted as reasonable all the criticisms of emigrants which appeared in the media, even those which were unjust or racist.

The third of the specific features I have attributed to current modes of experiencing guilt, experiencing it as a vague feeling, impossible to put a name to, all the more disturbing because indefinable, also appears in the four cases I am considering. Naturally there was always a feeling of having made a mistake, but not only that: the mistake was seen as having incalculable effects, even though not all of them had yet come to light, connected with impressions of indifference or dislike for what was most dear to them, of not really knowing oneself or life, of a general impossibility to make sense of today's world, inability to distinguish between reality and unreality . . .

How frequent are such cases of 'severe' guilt nowadays, and how are they affected by the sense of the absence of God?

On frequency I have no statistics, but I would venture to say that it is not low, in view of the current abundance of educational failures, disappointed youthful idealisms, destructive drug addictions and hopes placed in emigration and then bitterly frustrated.

As to how the absence of God might be affecting those who feel guilty I think we might achieve some clarity if we examine the mediations through which it has been possible and may be possible to work through feelings of guilt in a reasonably healthy way. This is what I shall try to do in the next section.

4. Mediations in the overcoming of guilt

It should not need saying that in this section I shall not be talking about overcoming those levels of guilt which from a clinical point of view are considered strictly pathological. The proper mediation for dealing in a healthy way with this pathological guilt is serious psychological or psychiatric treatment. Although it is frequently asserted that everything I have been calling 'severe guilt' always falls into this category, I do not think that this is so. Instead I regard as reasonable the assessment frequently made of themselves by quite a few people I have met: they experience a profound sense of guilt, but consider their distressing experience logical and not unhealthy. They would say that what is unhealthy is to go through what they are going through (having made a terrible mistake) and in spite of everything have no worries.

Having made this qualification, let us ask this question: in traditional societies which did not experience the current absence of God, what processes were generally used to achieve mental balance and stability after serious crises of self-accusation? And what perhaps essential psychological elements can be found in these ways of dealing with self-accusation?

The main written and oral accounts of those who had made great mistakes or great sinners who repented tell us something of what took place in those days, but primarily they show us what resources society believed could be used to tackle such cases. These mediations or resources recognized by society until recently can be reduced to three. A person could be saved by rituals (confession, sacrifices, penances . . .), or by deep experiences, in a sense mystical experiences, followed by dramatic changes of life: for example, a despotic master recognizes his error and begins to see the world with fresh eyes after a question from a child, or after seeing a small animal injured. The third case is where guilty persons were saved because someone was capable of loving them with a great love, greater than their wickedness (Don Juan Tenorio, according to the most popular version of his legend in Spain).

The association of feelings of guilt with these 'solutions' or possibilities of remedy in itself lessened the distress of feeling guilty. The psychological factor which made the most decisive contribution to this was beyond doubt the fact that the standard beliefs about ways of escaping from guilt situated guilt within a frame of reference in which it tended to be experienced as forming part of a history endowed with meaning and at least open to various solutions. Consequently it is normal that people who were initiated into that culture should find themselves affected individually and as a group when recourse to God becomes unavailable. Hemingway expressed this through one of his Republican characters in *For Whom the Bell Tolls* who had been involved in the cruel killing of members of the other side:

> After the war there will have to be some great penance done for the killing. If we no longer have religion after the war then I think there must be some form of civic penance organized that all may be cleansed from the killing or else we will never have a true and human basis for living.

There was something like these acts of civic penance here and there, for example in the Communist parties' self-purging processes, which put so much effort into getting the guilty to accuse themselves. However, even imagining these trials makes us ashamed: I am distressed at it, and if after episodes of guilt searches for a new personal and social balance had to be like that, then the absence of God would have terrible effects on those who experience guilt. At all events it would be necessary to explain why all this had to happen. Is Hemingway's character right when he says that once an individual has felt guilt they need some sort of penance, 'or else we will never have a true and human basis for living'?

To answer this question we must re-examine in more detail experiences of guilt and the symbolism of guilt.

5. Personal identity, time, the world of personal relations, guilt

The unease we feel when we feel guilty is not at root a shame in relation to others, though it usually produces this. It is something we feel in relation to ourselves; it is like seeing a deterioration in what we, even without explicitly admitting it, thought we were or wanted to be. Schopenhauer expressed this root feeling very well when he wrote that we don't really feel guilty when we say, 'How could I have done this?', but when we say to ourselves, 'What kind of person am I to have done this?'

In fact the last four words of the second question are superfluous, since there are people who feel guilty without knowing what for. We usually think that such feelings are absurd, but they exist and they show us something very important: that guilt is not merely the product of rational, conscious assessments. It arises in spite of us because we are tormented by the deterioration of something deep within us, which we know implicitly.

Of course this deterioration may damage us in terms of the post we occupy or in relation to the expectations others have of our work and friendship. But we may experience the fear of this damage without having a sensation of guilt; certainly this fear may make us ashamed of ourselves, but it is not identical with that feeling. Guilt, then, seems to be purely and simply a painful encounter with the fact that in our behaviour we are not as we thought we were or wanted to be. That is, it affects our personal identity. For our purposes there are two things we now have to explain: why it is painful, even very painful, to face the fact that we have acted out of what we thought was our character, and why as well as being painful it is disruptive and requires difficult treatment.

Let us start with the disruptive effect of guilt. A feeling of guilt occurs, I have been saying, when we think we have not acted in accordance with what we are or ought to be. However, what we implicitly regard as our character or our 'ideal self' is a sort of basic criterion in accordance with which we spontaneously give ourselves a place in our world of relationships and constantly organize our conduct, again spontaneously: we spontaneously do what is appropriate to this character of ours and in accordance with it we give ourselves a place in our everyday world.

Let us suppose that our image of what we are is completely disrupted. In this case we are unable to tell what is appropriate, we are completely confused, and the spontaneous direction of our behaviour is affected; we may have a crisis of identity.

Let us now imagine the case of guilt feelings. We have done something which does not correspond at all to the implicit idea we have of ourselves. The question arises, 'How could I have done this?' and the only answers which come are inadequate and irrational. On the one hand we think we know who we are, but on the other we find that we have not behaved in accordance with what we think is our character. What certainty can we have for action in the future? We have done something and wanted to do something which we now think was out of character, but if we wanted to do it it must have been in our character.

At the level of spontaneous consciousness we can no longer be sure of ourselves. Towards the future and at this spontaneous level time becomes strange for us, because we move towards it not knowing from what position we are going to look at things. Even the place we will spontaneously occupy among others becomes uncertain, because when our very identity changes or is called in question this upsets our implicit idea of our appropriate place among people and the solidarities and friendships we can expect. That is why we feel uneasy when we feel guilty, even when we reaffirm our transgressions: according to circumstances we may feel shame in relation to others, we may be ashamed of ourselves, feel self-pity, grief . . .

In view of all this we can say that at least two elements are important if the unease which is a natural component of feelings of guilt is not to be aggravated by excessive anxieties and obscurities. The first is that we should treat this identity whose spontaneous functioning is disrupted by guilt as inserted into a time frame which includes supports, a time frame in which, while there is no permanent guarantee of what we are, there is also never an end to the possibility of moving forward, and always the possibility of frames of references which guilt cannot attack. The other is spontaneously to sit loose to the system of relationships with others by which our identity is always defined: in this way other networks of relationships will always be available in which we can view ourselves, when because of guilt feelings we feel out of place in our usual network of personal relationships, in our family or the pattern of attitudes and behaviour organized around a particular ideology.

In cultures impregnated by the Judaeo-Christian tradition identity affected by guilt felt itself, above all in experiences of guilt, to be confronted with salvation and at the same time, sustained in this confrontation by God. This provided a temporal reference for individuals' self-image, and also populated the time frame with mediators and dispensers of possible help. Thus a person's own self-image incorporated a reference to a place and the openness of their own destiny to support from others. There was nothing alien about either 'life after guilt', which did not conjure up an image of uncertain situations, or those who occupied the time frame through which the guilty person would have to pass to rediscover themselves. This made it easier to deal with guilt.

6. In a culture which makes us feel God's absence

In our Western world it has not proved easy to secularize the model of innocence, guilt and redemption. It is obvious that those who have feelings of guilt but finds it ridiculous to think in terms of this model will suffer more in being left to exclusively to their own strengths and resources, when they may be only too painfully aware of their inadequacy. This also makes it logical for our age to repress guilt feelings no less than sexual feelings.

By repressing guilt, however, we do not cure the distress it causes, but simply move it somewhere else. One sign of this repression and displacement may be the enjoyment the public take in the exposure of guilt and guilty parties round about them, an enjoyment journalists know very well. In addition to this desperation to project guilt on to others, there is the rigidity which invades our self-image when it has been the negation mechanism which has stifled guilt feelings in advance; I think I see this type of rigidity in the way political groups deal with the grossest mistakes, and in the widespread social acceptance this procedure finds among their supporters.

I would like to say one thing. The sense of the absence of God may aggravate the secret distress of many people who experience feelings of guilt, and this will continue to happen as long as our culture does not make some secularized forms of the guilt-redemption model available to most people, if this is possible. But secret inner miseries are not the only result of the decline in society's ability to deal with guilt. This decline has social and political effects, and it is to be hoped that they will not make themselves felt in the scapegoating of weak minorities or countries by the strong or vice versa. This also has something to do with guilt.

Translated by Francis McDonagh

Death, the Ultimate Form of God's Silence

Pierre de Locht

I was consulted as a member of the *Concilium* section on spirituality about the plan for an issue on the theme 'Where is God?' In my reply I suggested 'an article on a certain silence of God in the last stage of life and then in the trial of death'. It was an article which should have been written by someone with a good deal of experience of being with dying people, a qualification which I certainly do not have. So I was amazed when the directors asked me to write on the topic. I was amazed and frightened, since to work on this theme compels one to dig deeper, to face oneself in a more personal way, to come to terms with what is the most mysterious part of human existence. For a long time I have had a personal intuition, an intuition which I expressed briefly in a book that I wrote more than twenty years ago (*Et pourtant je crois!*, 'And yet I believe!', Paris 1970); this intuition has steadily matured in me. So now I must make it more specific and draw it out, in some intensely personal questioning.

To talk of the 'silence of God' is already partly to prejudge the answer. People are surprised that God is silent at the crucial moment of death; or if God speaks, they ask why we do not grasp his word, without doubting either his existence or his presence. However, the silence of God can mask an even more basic possibility: the absence and in the last analysis the non-existence of God. So what we call the silence of God involves a double question, both why we do not perceive any word coming from God during this last phase, and whether this absence is not even the sign of a non-existence. Thus for the 'believer' as well, the ordeal of death perhaps consists at this final point in the fact that it implies a confrontation with essential solitude and possibly even with the perspective of nothingness. It is perhaps there that the last conscious gaze of the living person is directed.

We do not know anything about what is experienced in this last stage of existence. No one has come back to tell us. In the parable of the rich man and Lazarus, does not Jesus say that it would be useless for someone to come to speak to us of the other world, since we would not listen to him, and in any case we have signs to hand which can give us light (Luke 16.3)? The witness of those who, having approached death, often express their experience in terms of light, is by no means negligible. However, such evidence does not allow us to draw any conclusions about the experience of the ultimate transition which they have not made. The approach to death cannot be identified with death itself.

If it is impossible to have any idea about the conscious, existential content of this last phase, it is even more fallacious and vain to imagine how one might experience it. To attempt to prefigure it is to believe that one can take the sting out of the unknown and challenge the last adventure of existence.

Finitude, the condition in which we exist

It is important for me to accept the present reality, the only one of which I have a grasp. I have either to live with a latent, diffuse fear, often banished to the subconscious, or to recognize myself in the dimension of my personal existence, which is basically marked by finitude. I suppose that I am like everyone else in being constantly tempted to reject this finitude both in what I experience and undertake and in what binds me deeply to others. The important thing is to integrate the dimension of the limit, i.e. that part of finitude and death which is present in all human reality. To deny it or to pretend to ignore it is to falsify the truth and the quality of all experience.

Over the years I have been responsible for leading a working party on death. Around ten adults, from different backgrounds, have expressed in a non-directive context their apprehensions and desires, their perspectives on death – whether their own death or the death of their nearest and dearest. On each occasion these exchanges have brought us a renewed taste for and sense of life – life, moreover, perceived and accepted under the conditions and limits which mark out its contours, its weight, its price, its depths, its joy.

The human condition is a mysterious one. We constantly dream of perfection, plenitude, the infinite, and nevertheless can only make sense of our existence and build our happiness, bound up with that of others, in a reality which has inescapable conditions stamped upon it.

At a very early stage we experience and become aware of finitude. This happens the moment we perceive that we cannot do everything, that the simple fact of choosing a meal, a show, a profession, a more personal relationship, necessarily implies renunciations. These limitations press all the harder on those who have a handicap, whether transitory or permanent, those who are deprived of so many possibilities which others take for granted. And they press hard on all of us when we realize that our range of physical, intellectual and emotional capabilities is not unlimited. Think of all the things that we do to delude ourselves, hiding from ourselves these limitations and bounds which nevertheless define our identity!

A morality of unreality

The rejection of this finitude which alone constitutes our reality all too often underlies a certain presentation of so-called 'objective' morality which does not take fully into account every subjective approach (experienced by a subject), every decision taken in the realism of what is possible here and now. By rejecting the human condition as it is, and not as it is dreamed of, 'perfectionism', far from stimulating one's progress, paralyses and discourages. The perfection of a finite being is a task to accomplish in a rhythm personal to each individual. As Benjamin Franklin put it, 'On the day of my death I shall finally have ceased being born.' It is a matter of continuing indefatigably to model a personality: its principal elements are given to us, but they can only turn into a unique, personal being through what we forge in ourselves day after day. Life in its earthly course is a matter of being constantly on this way. And joy comes, not in the goal we achieve, so much as in the masterpiece of permanent creativity. You can read on the front of the Palais Chaillot in Paris: 'Every man creates without knowing it, just as he breathes. But the artist feels himself create. His act engages his whole being. His beloved pain strengthens it.' At certain moments every one is an artisan, an artist; we perceive ourselves as creators, even if only in apparently insignificant matters. Joy is possible, joy can be frequent, when we recognize and accept ourselves in our limited reality.

The illusions of infinity

We must also discover progressively that the quality of a commitment is not necessarily bound up with its definitive character. Here again, we must accept finitude and recognize that certain commitments can become meaningless if we seek to hold on to them come what may, even beyond their *raisons d'être*. In a way, setting a limit is each time a work of death. But is that not the condition of all human reality? If we ceaselessly dream of the infinite, do we not flee the demands of the real world in which we are involved? We may perhaps be doing so even when circumstances independent of our will impose these limits. In such cases we must submit to the limits. Otherwise we shall find it more difficult ourselves to take responsibility for certain limits. How many situations there are when we find that we have to choose – not out of egoism or a lack of generosity, as is too often believed, but simply in order to be attentive to the different values involved – solutions which inevitably have shadowy areas, solutions which are the lesser evil, but which in fact are good solutions in a precise situation! This is not situation ethics but ethics in a situation, an ethics linked with concrete reality which can only be experienced existentially.

To accept some limits, to accept death, is a demand made by moral maturity: we have to accept this and in some cases clearly choose it for the benefit of a more complete approach. No law, no external authority, can immediately settle this moral debate, which is often very intense. Does this not bring us to the nub of the tension which exists between a theoretical, 'objective' morality that makes statements by abstracting from existential circumstances and elements, and solutions decided consciously in the thick of situations which are always partly unique? One thinks of the great discussions about birth control (which was initially seen as an illegitimate limitation and rejection of life), contraception, artificial insemination, abortion, euthanasia . . . without prejudging so many other issues which will emerge sooner or later.

An ethic beyond ethics

So every ethical decision taken by the person implies an element of silence, of distance, of mystery: this region beyond the law, when the norms cannot follow the option to be taken right up to the ultimate decision; this region where all authority, however valid, is silent, where in the last analysis free and demanding responsibility plays a role. Here is a space which leaves room for and allows a completely personal commitment which, taking norms into account, takes on this extra task in the name of inner calls, which in the end are the most demanding.

An ethic supposed to be of Christian inspiration which, while claiming to bring the answer to any existential question, would suppress this last and decisive part of personal autonomy, would run counter to the most specific dimension of human responsibility. This is the permanent temptation for an institution which, thinking that it has to fill in the divine silences, brings ready-made answers to everything. By wishing to suppress the possibility of inadequate or 'bad' solutions, one removes the weight of personal autonomy which is indispensable if an attitude is to have a place in the moral sphere, i.e. is to be assumed in a responsible freedom. To act in a materially correct manner through submission is not sufficient for entering the moral sphere, for acting morally.

So this silence which is indispensable for allowing our existence as personal beings and not as individuals is essential for any authentically human ethic, regardless of whether or not it is inspired by Christianity. This is a silence that leaves room for precise orientations and decisions which in the last analysis devolve on the person and allow, or should allow, each one to raise himself or herself to the level of human dignity.

At the same time, at the heart of this solitude, there is a word, a presence: that of Jesus, which gives confidence, which relates the person to his or her autonomy, which gives us the audacity to dare to be ourselves, to be ourselves to the full. 'What do you think, Simon?' (Matt. 17.25); 'Why do you not judge me yourselves?' (Luke 12.57); 'Do not be afraid' (Matt. 14.22, 33); 'Who do you say that I am?' (Matt. 16.15); 'Take up your bed and walk' (John 5.8). And already, to Abraham, 'Go to yourself' (Gen. 12.1).

Only when the moral authorities, whatever they may be, are silent, is the way opened up to this part which is the most specifically human part of our personal careers: where it is necessary to opt, in the last analysis, in responsible and free autonomy; to make choices, to accept limits, parts of death without which nothing can be built. And neither Jesus nor the Spirit of Jesus come to fill this silence with a normative word or with constraining calls. Could it not be broken by words causing uncertainty because they are uncertain?

Decline and openness

The richer one becomes in years, to take up the term used for the patriarchs, the more the awareness of one's own finitude grows. One's grip on events slackens, and dear ones disappear. Everything one holds on to, for which one fights, everything that interests one – all this will continue after me, without me. How will the church, the Christian faith develop, which today are dear to my heart and to which I devote the best of myself? What will become of all that I have worked for, about which I am so enthusiastic? What will become of those who are near to me, who make me what I am? I shall no longer have any grip on all that.

However, from now on I want to remain alive, detaching myself little by little from this way of involving myself in commitments, relationships, as though nothing had to stop. The perception of finitude increasingly marks my existence. Is this an amputation or access to more truth? Are the commitments, the events, the beings, less valuable because they are not immutable, imperishable, and will go on without me? Do I narrow myself or grow in truth when I recognize and as far as possible accept myself as a being basically marked by transitoriness in this universe, the only one that I know, or have I learned and do I continue to learn, to exist personally?

Finitude and resurrection

Since I encounter the agnostic world in a personal way, and since I appreciate the honesty and the profoundly human feelings of some of those people who have no faith in an other world beyond humankind, I have come to feel one particular question keenly: how do we live out, integrate, cultivate, belief in the resurrection without escaping the dimension of finitude inherent in the human person? Do we not run the risk of defusing the confrontation with finitude by too immediate a recourse to eternity? Do we not glide over the confrontation with the limits, with all the realities of the death of everyday human life?

As is suggested by the juxtaposition of the two sayings 'My God, my God, why have you forsaken me?' (Matt. 27.46) and 'Father, into your hands I commend my spirit' (Luke 23.46), Jesus himself experienced this tension. The first Christian community partly escaped it through its belief in an imminent parousia, as a result of which it was entirely concentrated on something outside this world. The twenty centuries of Christianity are marked by this permanent friction between the present reality, which has to be taken completely seriously, and establishing a distance from the 'world', from a universe the sole significance of which is to prepare for heaven. For example, to justify holy celibacy or even sexual abstinence by a married couple as an anticipation of future realities shows the difficulty – which we shall probably never completely surmount – of living out our entire responsibility for the present realities through belief in the resurrection.

A finitude which prepares us for welcoming

If all human beings are creators, if they progressively conquer their autonomy, if they are rightly set on responsible freedom, it is important for them to discover at the same time that they only exist and can only fulfil themselves in relationship to others, in welcoming those who are different. The relationship that theology has always demonstrated as forming part of the very essence of the triune God is just as essential for the human person. We exist only in relationship, and it is at the heart of this relational universe that each of us constructs his or her identity. Availability, welcoming, are thus constitutive of the person. In a world which is increasingly based on competition, in which the other is so often threatening, or fear henceforth gnaws at us, it is important to know how to trust, how to continue – in realism and lucidity – to have faith in others. It is lifegiving for them and vital for us. We only create ourselves, we only truly blossom, where we dare to have confidence, when we discover that attention to others, welcoming those who are different, is not only a generous act but also an indispensable truth for existing as a being in relation.

There is a long apprenticeship of dialogue in trust. Far from robbing us of ourselves, relationships shape us. We form ourselves through welcoming others. Religious faith lies in the same perspective, if it has got beyond the spectre of a vengeful, angry, threatening God and in the light of the gospel has set faith above duties, in the sphere of love.

Attaching supreme value all our lives to a trusting welcoming of both others and God does not prevent us from having to construct ourselves, to rely on our strength, to assume our responsibilities. We constantly have to find a right balance between availability and being in control in a most personal way. What is true in respect of others is *a fortiori* true in respect of God, the God of Jesus Christ who wants us to be free and capable of autonomous decisions, who wants us to stand upright.

So that there is only trust

I am less and less sympathetic to the idea that death is the consequence of sin. I see it as being inherent in the created, incarnate condition. For the believer, will not the final stage of life, marked by its growing limits, its increased dependence on others up to the point of death, which from some points of view would seem scandalous to a living being endowed with conscience, have a primordial significance? I ask myself whether this last phase of existence, in which we can no longer do anything by ourselves, in which we are totally dependent, is not indispensable if we are to open ourselves to the fullness of God.

At this stage, everything takes place in silence. Our personal assumption of responsibility, our merits and virtues, our so-called 'rights' to a recompense, and even our ideas about the beyond, about an eternal bliss – all that no longer has any weight. The silence, and even perhaps a certain silence of God, is necessary so that at this point there is only trust. There is no other viaticum or provision for the journey. It is a matter of having trust, a trust which nothing obscures, encumbers, weakens, limits. Trust pushed to extremes. For finally, in the face of God there is only welcoming, a full welcoming. Any restriction to this welcoming that any connection with merits or whatever might bring, would pose some obstacle to absolute trust.

In the image of the triune God

At this last phase of existence, I am called on in particular to join in the filial abandonment of Christ. One way of understanding the Trinity, very much based in the theological tradition, might seem capable of illuminating this last stage of existence. The Word can only be as just as equally and fully God as the 'Father', the primary source, is God, while at the same time being distinct, if he does not want to be self-sufficient in anything and totally welcomes the plenary gift. If in anything whatsoever the Son wanted to be independent, if there was anything in him that was not received, welcomed being, he would not be as totally God as the 'source'. Similarly, the Father would not be completely Father if he kept back anything whatsoever. Here we have the perfect communication of the fullness of being, possessed in different ways, whether as given or as received, but also existing, to the degree that there is no reserve in this perfect communication either from the side of the gift or from the side of the welcoming.

Granted, this is a clumsy way of putting it, but it is one which perhaps makes an essential point both about our condition, as being created in the image of God, and the significance of death. All along our earthly career we are forming ourselves as personal beings, with a unique identity. At the end of this adventure, at the threshold of coming 'face to face' with the infinite, surely only a filial receptivity will make any sense. Now the time for self-sufficiency is gone. By his life and his teaching, Jesus of Nazareth initiated us into a filial attitude. There is no more in this last phase than being son or daughter, totally accepting our filial condition, henceforth no longer engaged in creative action: here there is nothing for us but to open ourselves without limit to trust, to faith. Not faith in the 'trust which must be believed', in our merits or those of the church, but a faith entirely centred on God. Because he is God, God with us and for us. If there is God, I can only attain the 'face to face' by abandonment.

In this same perspective, it becomes difficult for me to affirm certainties about death, the beyond. To be certain is still to find in oneself and in the human condition reasons, justifications, guarantees, proofs. It is less and less a matter of certitude and more a matter of a hope which is purified and taken to its extreme. In hope there is an abandonment, an attitude of complete trust, trust supported by these germs of eternity which already mark our present way.

It seems to me that if it is important that in this last phase, the *pausa longa* of earthly existence, for trust in God to be the only vital leaven, it is important at the same time for those who are dying, having been invited to show the most open trust possible, to be surrounded by those warm human relationships which evoked trust, invited trust, accustomed them to trust during the course of their earthly lives.

The silence demanded by this ultimate phase is above all silence in ourselves: the silencing of all that has animated us, made us fit, creative; the silencing also of all our ideas of God, our images of the beyond, what we feel owed for our virtues, the reckoning of our faults and our merits. The silencing of all that through which we – and too often the institutional church – have a tendency to reassure ourselves or to disturb ourselves, so that all that is left is confident expectation.

Is this also the silence of God? Who can say? At all events, our silence, made up solely of abandonment, is indispensable if we are to leave room for God, who alone can give meaning, life, joy to this passing – to this Easter.

Translated by John Bowden

The Metaphor of God

Yves Cattin

Talk of God permanently runs the risk of being either illusion or invocation, so it seems to me to be useful, at the beginning of this study, to spell out the limits of my reflection.

I do not want to take up the old debate on the being of God and the names which we can give him. Nor shall I try to analyse the experiences people can have of God. More modestly, and short of these important questions, I shall attempt to reflect on what is constantly presupposed by them and often passes unnoticed, i.e. on the 'place' of a possible encounter with God. For human beings to begin to talk of God, for them to have a relationship with God, it is important, first, for them to encounter God 'somewhere'. This place of encounter is essential at this point, in that it determines the validity of all rational discourse about God and all words of invocation. It is presupposed by all the religions as what makes them possible, and it is probably postulated, as Pascal suggests, by all questions about God.

However, in meditating on this place of a possible encounter with God I am not attempting to retrace the course of a hypothetical proof of God. In this proof, reason tests the coherence of its own functioning while at the same time examining more widely the coherence of human experience. Reason never encounters God, but postulates God as the horizon of this experience. The language born of proof always speaks of an absence and not of an encounter; it states an absolute which we always lack.

The place where Transcendence encounters finitude can only be a metaphorical place. Here I understand metaphor in the etymological and original sense of a 'transport' in which the Transcendent offers itself to be encountered by human beings who welcome it freely. Transcendence remains transcendent; the God encountered is the true God. And the human being who encounters God is a human being who is not constrained to abandon his or her humanity in this encounter. So this metaphorical place is never imaginary; it is a historical place where the true God encounters human beings, while allowing them to be human beings.

1. The idol as a common place

Before and outside all reflection, before all metaphor, human beings have given, and still give, themselves a common place with God. They give themselves an idol.

With a long Jewish-Christian tradition behind us, we move too quickly in our criticism of idols. Before being a false, naive or archaic god, the idol reveals the seriousness and the tragic gravity of human existence. And if it is the somewhat derisory invention of an impotent god, here nevertheless human beings give themselves a space for encountering God. In the distance which separates them from God and seems intolerable to them, they yield to the temptation of proximity and make themselves the idol of God.

The process of inventing an idol is complex, and we cannot examine it here. In their desire to exist, human beings test both sense and finitude. And in this contradiction of a finite sense, a positivity achieved in the face of the non-sense signified in death, desire imprisons itself in the circularity of the self. It becomes a desperate perseverance in being. Here we have the source of an original violence which turns the desire to exist into a desire for death and murder. That is the birthplace of the idol. To break this vicious circle, human beings invent a sacred space which averts violence by limiting it. The sacral is at the same time the place of the norm imposed on desire, and the space for the symbolic realization of this same desire. Human beings invent for themselves a useful transcendence which will allow both a negotiated realization of desire and social cohesion.

But this invention of the sacred space of the idol is not without its consequences for human existence. The banning of the idol involves this existence in an insuperable contradiction. The desire to exist can be realized only by accepting in advance that one is measured by that which is other than oneself, and the idol establishes the human being in a state of servitude. Desire, creator of meaning, is never master of meaning. And the idol, fascinating and terrifying, is an *alter ego* that devours the self which has brought it into being. Concrete human existence founders on this symbolic realization which the idol brings about in the sphere of the sacred. This god, experienced in the form of that which is near and alike, this god within range of voice and mouth, takes human beings hostage and strips human history of all that is serious and solemn. We have only to re-read the *Iliad* to convince ourselves of this. The real history is enacted between Athene, Apollo and the gods of Olympus, and not between the Trojans and the Achaeans, who tried desperately to escape their manipulation. Time and history get lost in mythology, because of the removal of every stake in human freedom.

But there is a twofold lesson in this failure of the idol. First of all, in human experience, there is a certain naturality of God. By that I mean that human beings, in their desire to exist, feel the need of God as a condition for the possibility of realizing their humanity. And in this sense one can say that human beings invent God in order to become human. But on the other hand, in this need for God which leads them to make idols, human beings always come to grief. The idol is an absent god, a god for want of God. And if the idol does not consent to this recognition, if it persists in acting as the true God in too close a proximity, then it destroys human beings and their responsible freedom.

We need to meditate on this lesson that idols teach us. When human beings desire to encounter God in the kind of proximity that robs God of all transcendence, then they miss the true God and encounter only their own image. And at the same time they renounce their historical freedom and responsibility. Everything goes on as if the affirmation of the transcendence of God were the supreme guarantee of the humanity of human beings and their freedom. That is the most profound teaching of the history of idols and their failure.

2. The gods subjected to reason

It was this failure of the idols that philosophy denounced when it appeared in Greece. At that time it undertook a radical critique of the idols of religion. It was not that philosophy wanted to suppress religion and the gods. As Socrates said to his judges, 'I believe in them more than any of my accusers' (*Apology* 35d). In its reflection, philosophy seeks to establish the truth of religion. And its critique primarily bears witness to a concern for the transcendence of God. Thus Plato drove the poets out of the city to preserve the divinity of the gods.

Now paradoxically, this concern to think of the highest transcendence of God destroys such transcendence. Unless it in effect affirms that the concept of God makes no sense, philosophy must try to think out this concept and the reality that it denotes, and it does so on the basis of what makes sense for it, the intelligibility of the world. Philosophy then finds itself faced with an insoluble dilemma. Either the transcendence of God is thought of on the basis of the system of which it becomes the central and basic element. In that case, in making up a system with the world, this God loses all transcendence, and the concept of God no longer has any critical power, because God no longer has any otherness and becomes incapable of being present with a real presence. That is the case of the god of Aristotle, the Stoics, Spinoza or Hegel. Or philosophy tries desperately to maintain the supreme transcendence, in which case it is impotent to speak of it and is thus led to renounce itself by establishing itself in silence.

I cannot embark on a critical account of philosophical discourse on God here, but I nevertheless want to recall certain limits.

1. A concern for the transcendence of God leads philosophy, in its criticism of the idol of a God who is too close, to uproot the desire from the need that it has for the Absolute, to purify this desire by extending it to infinity and stripping it of all the intermediaries which it invents for itself. Thus philosophy can clearly see what is lacking in the idol and what prevents it from being a true God, namely transcendent otherness. But what it then forgets is what the idol gives despite its imperfection, namely the presence of a god whom human beings encounter. Thus uprooted from the concrete existence which inspires it, desire without desire no longer has any human space in which to realize itself. It ceases to be desiring, or it leads people to renounce the world, history and philosophy for an ineffable adventure in an abyss which swallows people up in a kind of fascination with nothingness.

2. If philosophy does not accept this abyss and does not renounce itself and its demand for rationality, then the philosopher who rejects the idols of the people runs the risk of inventing another idol, that of the system. And this idol is even poorer and more impotent than the others, since it can never become the space for an encounter with God. This god of the philosophers lacks any condescension towards human beings, who can scarcely direct their desires towards it. The god of Plato is the impersonal idea of the Good; the god of Aristotle is a thought which thinks itself. And Hegel's encyclopaedia ends up with a deity which is indifferent to the world of human beings, a divinity which is the achievement of philosophy.

3. If nevertheless the philosopher undertakes not to renounce an encounter with the transcendent God, he or she is led to renounce philosophy itself, as is shown by the history of pagan and Christian neo-Platonisms. Desire, dispossessed of any human context, undertakes an impossible pilgrimage beyond the world. Finitude is interpreted as a

fall, an illusion or a fault, and philosophy becomes the description of a return to God accomplished in nostalgia. Man is a deficient being whom only reconciliation with the unity of God as a totality beyond the world can bring to fulfilment. The world and history are abandoned to violence and meaninglessness in favour of another world, the only real world, which human beings seek desperately to achieve.

4. So philosophy is incapable of thinking of a metaphor of God which would authorize a real encounter between the true God and living man. Its more modest task is nevertheless necessary: indefatigably, philosophy denounces all the common places of God. But it always fails to realize the presence of God and to decipher the signs of this presence. If, while refusing to put God in the explicative order of things, despite everything it attempts to realize his presence, then God is present in the world and history in an insignificant way, in a beyond out of reach and out of hearing. The Absolute may well manifest itself for itself *in* the finite, but it never manifests itself *to* the finite. For philosophy, human beings are never before God, in a face-to-face encounter, but are in God, or irremediably separated from him. I think that in one way or another philosophy always brings God into the order of the system or totality, just as it brings the living human being into this order. In this order, our loves and our pains, our miseries, our despairs and our joys dissolve. There they take on meaning. But they never have the meaning that they have in our lives. The desire of the living human being to encounter the living God is similarly lost. And in the solemnity of finitude the vocation of human beings to enter into covenant and association with the living God is never perceived.

Thus in its utmost rigour, as Merleau-Ponty asserted, philosophy is the most radical atheism, the most resolute assertion of the absence of God, and at best the wound of this absence. However, this failure is its success. Unmasking the doubtful subjectivities which claim too easy a proximity to God, it is the introduction to an effort to purify desire and thought. God is then pointed to as belonging to the order of freedom. That is beyond question the most profound lesson of philosophy.

3. Loving the Torah more than God

In its affirmation of a revelation of God coming to offer a covenant to human beings, Judaism describes a historic space for the encounter with God. The covenant establishes a possible way of living with God, the condition for which is faith. In fact the covenant and the encounter with God are not given as the fulfilment of human experience. That lies in the impossibility of God, and in this sense Judaism confirms the failure of philosophy. The covenant introduces human beings to the experience of free gift, and the encounter with God does not relate primarily to the ontological order, but has its place and expresses itself in a history of love and mercy. It is also an evocation of human freedom. It forbids human beings to dream subjectively of ecstatic experience, and calls on them to make a historical commitment in fidelity.

There without doubt is the supreme originality of Judaism. The encounter with God is not in the order of discourse or even mystical experience, but is realized in the practice of the law, the Torah: it is the ethical obligation of justice. The practice of the Torah, which is the word of God that creates our humanity, brings about the election of the believer for the encounter with God. The obligation of holiness and praise is the obligation of justice towards the other person. This tension that Judaism introduces into the social relationship by making it the place of the manifestation of God gave birth to messianism as a recapitulation of history and human time interpreted as a sacred history and a divine time. In this eschatological hope, each believer must accept the time of justice by becoming messiah.

This explains the obstinate rejection of all idols in Judaism. The Holy One, whom one cannot name and whom no human being can see without dying, can only be encountered in the practice of the Torah, in the recognition of others. And it is necessary really to 'love the Torah more than God', as an anonymous sage put it, since it is the place of the manifestation of the transcendence of God. By recognizing others in the proximity of the neighbour, by renouncing violence and murder, the believer enters into the freedom which is the very freedom of God. The place of encounter with God is thus a true place, a human place, the face of the other, and there we are called to ethical responsibility. And at the same time it is a non-place where the transcendence of God is given to us not to see, but to hear. In this vocation, localized in this way, human beings are directed to history and freedom, and they must become creators as God is the Creator.

So the encounter with God is not thought or felt, but realized and acted out in the very act of responsible freedom. The supreme gift, the encounter with the holy God, is also that which has to be done, the practice of justice. And reciprocally this ethical practice comes to be identified as the encounter with the holy God in the signs of belonging to the chosen people, in a ritual practice. Then the face of the other is fully shown to be a place where the transcendence of God is manifested.

Historically, Judaism became established in the fertile tension between the practice of justice in a universal responsibility and the obligation to show this practice, in the rites of the Temple, as being the proximity of the transcendent God. And the election is lived out under the twofold mode of a call to universal responsibility and the affirmation of a social and religious particularism. Thus, as a midrash relates, the mummy of the one who obeys rigorously goes before the ark of the one who lives eternally.

What makes the greatness of Judaism is also its limit. And in my view this limit is that of thinking of the encounter with God in terms of an election inscribed on the physical body by circumcision and on the social body by the ritual code. Despite its intention of universality, this physical and social inscription limits the space of the manifestation of God by codifying a greater or lesser proximity to the neighbour. It is for this that Jesus never ceased to reproach the doctors of the law. This amounts to a refusal to accede completely to the absolute gratuitousness of the coming of God and to want still to imprison him in human frameworks, however religious.

But in Judaism there is a movement to go beyond this sociological enrolment, that of belonging to God. This movement is denoted by the expectation of the Messiah, the expectation of the hour when all the nations enter into the Israel of God. This is the hour that Jesus proclaims as having come.

4. 'Image of the invisible God'

Christianity, taking up Judaism, brings about a radicalization which it presents as a fulfilment of Judaism.

Judaism put the encounter with God in the face of the other person, towards whom I have to practise justice. Christianity fulfilled this metaphor by affirming that God is incarnate in a particular historical person, Jesus of Nazareth. Thus the covenant is fulfilled and made perfect, and God enters history in the most unthinkable way. The word of revelation then becomes a living and historical word in this Christ who is confessed as Son of God. So God is definitively located in the history of the world, in the humanity of this man who is God.

The consequence of this is that in this man Jesus, the humanity of every human being, called to become sons, becomes the holy place of the manifestation of God in this world. It is not that every human being is God. But the humanity of every human being is the place of the manifestation of God in this world, the place where they are elected to communion with God. The Jewish affirmation is then realized and the critique of idols is accomplished. The sacred is no longer in the world, or in things, far less beyond the world. It is in the humanity of each human being, a humanity which is fulfilled in the humanity of Jesus. The election of Israel becomes truly universal: there is no longer Jew nor Greek nor slave nor free, but only human beings called to their humanity in the encounter with God.

But in this way Jesus brings about a radical break with Judaism, by offering a new way of belonging to God. This belonging is no longer mediated by the practice of the Torah but with reference to Jesus himself, to the humanity of God in him. So Jesus abandons the textual corpus of the Torah which was what held Israel together, and all men and women are called on to define themselves in relationship to him, to Jesus. However, this belonging is realized only if Jesus is confessed in faith as Christ. If Jesus were only a human being, his claim would be blasphemous, as his contemporaries saw quite clearly. This new belonging destroys the positivity experienced in the practice of the Torah by Judaism, which in this way brought about a degree of proximity to God. Jesus destroys this positivity in two ways, and that explains the disarray of the first disciples. On the one hand the reference to the Torah no longer comes first – what counts is the recognition of Jesus as Christ, master of the Torah. And on the other hand, Jesus leaves his disciples, and they have to experience his absence, in remembrance of him.

This apprenticeship to the memory of Jesus was to bring about a second radicalization, as essential renewal of the ethical obligation inscribed in the Torah, which is not destroyed but fulfilled. In the remembrance of Christ, belonging to God is no longer signified only by the practice of the law which guarantees balanced relationships in the social body. It is signified in the absolute of the law, absolute dedication to the humanity of all human beings, taken into the humanity of Christ as the place of the manifestation of God. This absolute dedication, this devotion to others, turns the obligation of justice into an obligation of love. The absence of Jesus, of whom they maintain the remembrance, obliges believers to realize the presence of Christ and God in their relation to others. That is the meaning of the Sermon on the Mount, which bases the ethical obligation of love as the perfection of the law on the obligation for the believer to be perfect and holy as the heavenly Father is perfect and holy.

Thus belonging to others becomes the place of belonging to God, as is clearly indicated by Matthew 25. And human beings encounter God only if they are entirely dedicated to others. This transcending of the Law is not a 'utopian impatience' which frees from ethical obligation by abandoning the world to injustice and violence. On the contrary, this obligation to love emphasizes that the relationship with the other to whom justice must be done can be the place of the encounter with God only if this relationship enters the sphere of overflowing and apparently useless gratuitousness, over and above what is due. Not only must believers observe the law, but they are called to the freedom of the love which is shown by God. The concern of justice is a concern of love. It is necessary not only to give but even to give without getting anything in return. Then human beings act 'as God acts'.

So all human beings are called to a creative and responsible freedom, a freedom critical of immediate advantage, of the imperatives of survival and social convenience. And the story of Jesus, which is the story of God's action, indicates the kind of life lived by this person who manifests God. It is that of the suffering servant, the one who accepts death for others. Then the supreme transcendence of God is shown.

5. The other and his or her face

Can the theologian or the philosopher think out this way in which God is revealed in the face of the other person? Can they think the unthinkable? Here thought seems to be confronted with an insoluble dilemma: either I affirm the positivity of the other; I stop with him or her, recognizing them for who they are and only for who they are. In that case I do not see God, who is then a pure nothingness of thought. Or I want to see God, and this desire takes me through the other person, whose face becomes transparent, so that I no longer recognize the other: his or her irreducible otherness disappears before my gaze.

Both Judaism and Christianity indicate the direction in which we must look to get over this apparent dilemma. I can only really take the face of the other into account, while at the same time this face becomes the place where I encounter God, if I maintain a particular relationship of justice and mercy with the other. So it is not just any relationship with the other which manifests God. But one can also add that it is not just any relationship which manifests the other person as the other. In an ethical relationship, the truth of the relationship to others is the truth of the manifestation of God. That does not mean that the other person is God, nor is this just a way of talking. It indicates that the ethical relationship to the other person is the metaphor of God: in this relationship to the other person I am 'experiencing' (in a sense which I shall explain in due course) the presence of God. This implies first of all that I have a true relationship with the other, and then that I can have a true relationship with God outside this true relationship with the other. And faith will add that the reverse is true, that I can only have a true relationship with the other through the gift of God who has made me in his image.

This indication for thought then raises two problems. First of all we have to know what is a true relationship to the other person; or, if you like, who this other whom I meet really is. The second problem is to know how this relationship manifests God, what this God is who is encountered in the face of the other.

The other becomes the other only when he or she ceases to be a thing for me. As long as the other is only a thing, I am only an 'I' in a world of things that I manipulate to my taste or that I suffer reluctantly. In that case the desire to exist clears a way for itself by reducing all otherness. This is the world of reductive violence. Also, the other person is only recognized as other when I renounce this violence and accept an ethical obligation. Then the other in every respect spills over the idea I have of him or her and it proves impossible to reduce him or her to thought or manipulation. Because I feel an obligation in the face of the other, he or she always goes beyond where I am. In an unpredictable way, the other prevents me from adding up the world as my world, and it is in recognizing my obligation to the other that I receive from him or her the fact of being more than I am.

In fact this recognition of the other introduces me to a new type of existence. Instead of existing with, or alongside, I begin to exist in front of the other, or more exactly, face to face. And it is for this reason that the other person who is encountered is always a face.

This face-to-face encounter resists fusion or confusion and always maintains the otherness by separation. And the only way of maintaining this otherness by preserving it from violence is an ethical relationship in which I recognize a commitment to justice. When the face of the other appears before me, I recognize that I have no power. The other escapes the system of my world and enters this world as a stranger who becomes my guest and for whom I become responsible. Then, by the intermediary of the things that belong to my world, I am invited to offer to the other the hospitality that I owe to him or her. This is the only kind of power I have when I see the other's face. That is, unless I yield to the temptation of murder in some form, the result of which is that the other, who is not a thing, is no longer anything.

When I am faced with the other, no interiority can serve as a refuge or an excuse for me. It is no longer 'up to me', but I exist under an obligation, as though broken by the presence of the other that I recognize. So my freedom is put in question by the other, and this is the only question which counts as far as I am concerned, since it is my being which is at stake here, in this summons to responsibility and justice. We have to go still further, and say that in the recognition of the face of the other, and of my obligation towards him or her, I am shown my own humanity and the whole of humanity in the proclamation of a sociality and a brotherhood for which I am required. So the face of the other is already prophetic: it speaks to me of the whole of humanity.

Thus the face of the other is not just the face of the other whom I love. The other is the other human, whoever he or she may be, perhaps my enemy, who assumes a face, becomes the place where I choose my obligation to humanity.

6. The visitation of the face

The Jewish and Christian scriptures affirm that it is in this event of the other, which is always an ad-vent, that the encounter with God takes place. And we have to ask what becomes visible in the face of the other person.

To assert that the other is recognized in an ethical relationship is to state the concrete and historical character of this encounter with the other. The other is encountered in his or her situation, history, joy and misery, and I become obliged to them in an obligation to all humanity. So this encounter is a true encounter with a real other, and each time the ethical task is unique and unpredictable. I am truly face to face with the other in a kind of vertical horizontality which defines the ethical obligation.

To say that this is the way in which I encounter God is to suggest that in thus coming face to face with the other I encounter God obliquely and not face to face, since it is this other whom I encounter face to face. Unless I say that the other is God, I do not know how to encounter God face to face. So the other does not make God *visible*; I see and continue to see only the other. But in this face that I recognize, God begins to speak and becomes *audible*. This happens in the space of the conversation where the other becomes a face for me. God becomes a speaker.

Here we have to remember what I have just said about the absence of Christ and the remembrance of him in which the believer exists and which makes possible what Matthew 25 affirms: 'I was hungry and you gave me food, I was thirsty and you gave me drink, I was a stranger and you welcomed me, I was naked and you clothed me, I was a prisoner and you visited me' (35f.). In my experience of the face of the other, an experience which is wholly human and limited, faith makes me decipher an 'experience' of God of which it is difficult to give any account in rational terms.

The other is encountered as the other in his or her face. But this face veils an invisible presence which begins to speak. So the face of the other is his or her face and is more than that face; it is a face which is visited.

How can we think of this visitation of the face of the other? The other becomes a face for me only in the ethical relationship that I establish with him or her. And it is in this ethical obligation that I have access to the Transcendence which visits the face of the other. In fact, in this face which lays an obligation on me, what is seen is the visible, i.e. this person whose neighbour I become. But if this face lays an obligation on me, it is because it begins to speak with a word which does not come from the person concerned but from beyond him or her, from a Transcendence which visits them and manifests itself as a face. Moreover, I am not the one who constitutes the other as a face, any more than he or she gives themselves a face; a face is given to the other in the same way as the obligation of ethical recognition is given to me. We both exist in this original gift which brings us together into the experience of the gratuitousness of being *human*. And when I recognize my obligation to others, when I hear (*audire*) a word spoken in the face of this other, and obey (*obaudire*) this word that I have heard, God, whom no one can see without dying, exposes himself in the face of the other person at the very moment when this face is disguising him by manifesting the other person.

So the face which manifests the other person reveals the transcendent God. This face accosts me by crying out its strangeness to the world, its wretchedness and its death. And it commits me to justice in the perfection of love. This is in no way a vague feeling of pity, but an obligation imposed on my freedom. So in the face of the other there is a strange authority which is both imperative and disarmed. And this authority does not come from the other, who has no more claim to such authority than I do. It comes from God, who visits this face.

Thus the presence of God is not experienced in the proper sense of the term, and I shall never be able to say that the other person is God for me. But this presence is effectuated in the act in which, face to face with the other, I recognize that I am obligated to justice. However, I can only achieve this recognition because the transcendence of God reveals itself in the other person and gives him or her a face. So the revelation of the transcendence of God in the face of the other is what obligates me to justice, but I have to realize this revelation of God concretely in the work of justice. This paradox of the faith which is purely gratuitous but is also an obligation to works seems to be the constitutive paradox of the humanity of everyone who has to become freely human in the constantly renewed gift made to him or her of humanity in relation to others. But perhaps this paradox, which appears when the creative transcendence of God encounters the responsible freedom of the human person, is unsurmountable for us only because one of the two terms, the transcendence of God, always escapes us.

So I obey the authority of a word which can be heard in the face of the other. But if this word is imperative because it is a sign of transcendence, the presence which is manifested there remains veiled for me. As rabbinic wisdom says, 'Wherever the exaltation of God is expressed, there already his humility is proclaimed'. I do not see God face to face; I do not see anything, but this nothing speaks to me and lays upon me an obligation to the other. The Jewish and Christian traditions have been almost obsessed with this 'experience' of a nothing which has the fullness of a presence, and they have tried to give an account of it with all the means at their disposal, as if one could speak of an experience which is not an experience.

And just as the knowledge of the other does not reveal the other to me as other, but as a thing, and it is only in the relationship of ethical responsibility that the other is recognized in his or her face, so God is not known and experienced in the face of the other. But he is recognized and encountered in the very act in which I recognize the other as transcendence and obligation for me. What is really experienced is the encounter with the other in the renunciation of violence and the practice of justice. But if I thus truly encounter the other, then my relationship which stops at this other cannot stop in him or her. It puzzles over an empty fullness which makes me glimpse the secret of the face of the other. And as Kierkegaard says, this secret is all the more secret when it is exposed in a public place. Attentive to this secret, I then hear the echo of a word which lays upon me an obligation to justice. So what is signified in this experience is that I encounter the transcendence of God, of whom I never have any experience. This encounter is never felt, and I can never say it except in describing its trace in the states of my active subjectivity. For this encounter which is not felt must nevertheless be permanently verified in the practice of justice. The experience of this nothingness which visits the face of the other thus rests on a nothingness of experience in which there is a revelation of a transcendent fullness that puts me under an obligation to the other and to all humanity. This is the paradox of the revelation of the transcendent God who speaks by giving me the word of responsibility. But this word constantly overflows into the word which calls me to justice, so that I am never finished with ethics.

Such an encounter cannot be put into words, but it engenders a surfeit of words in invocation and praise; it gives birth to the poem as a constantly reiterated attempt to express an ineffable presence and proximity, the poem which speaks an impossible word. Then the work of justice becomes a work of pure contemplation, celebration of the presence which visits the face of the other, in the obstinate rejection of the ever-present temptation to fusional immediacy.

Nevertheless, if discourse fails to express the transcendence encountered, thus accepting the impossibility of a true 'theology', it can still describe the conditions and the consequences of this manifestation of God in the life of human beings, in a kind of 'anthropology of God', of which, in Christianity, christology remains the model and the norm.

7. The anthropology of God

To end this study I would like briefly to indicate some themes for reflection on this anthropology of God.

1. That the other is always the unique metaphor for me, that the other is always mediated in his or her advent by the work of justice, is the mark which guarantees the supreme transcendence of God. God always escapes the grasp of my thought and my action: I can never encounter God through possession; it is always through gift and grace. The manifestation of the supreme transcendence of God is that of love freely given. Thus the work of justice is a permanent invitation to fulfilment in love and praise.

That brings to its conclusion the conversion of the desire which makes idols. In the recognition of its obligation towards the other, desire must consent to cease to be a mechanism of identity, reducing the other to an object of possession. Desire is invited to detach itself from the need that the self has to fill its void in order to enter into the recognition of the other as homage and obligation. Then desire ceases to use its own criteria and consents to the unboundedness of the other, which is only the unboundedness of the transcendence which visits his or her face. Then the desire which stops at the other does not stop there; it is breathed by the desirable without desire; it forgets what it originally lacked in the encounter with the one who lacks nothing. The uncrossable distance which separates me from the Wholly Other is thus in a way crossed: the desire becomes desire without desire; it renounces being for being by consenting to be for the other. Then it enters into the recognition of God.

2. The God whom I then encounter bears witness to an infinite respect for human freedom. Renouncing the violence of the sacral, it offers itself by leaving me free to encounter it. I am neither ravished nor annihilated by contact with it, any more than the face of the other is annihilated by its visitation. I am no longer transported outside myself or my life. I am myself, and I remain myself. I do not begin to participate in the being of the Transcendent in an ineffable fashion, but I enter into relation with him. Renouncing the mythical universe of a participation in the divine, and having become an atheist about all the gods, I enter into history with God. I become a believer in the sense that I renounce the illusory proximity of the face to face and enter into an infinite hermeneutic of the face of the other, which gives signs of the presence of the God who is always absent. Then I hear a word which makes me responsible for this presence, in the work of justice and peace.

3. So it is always the face of the other which is the metaphor of God. And the God recognized in this face always sends me back to my responsibility to human beings and things. My relationship to God is therefore always a social relationship. The holy and transcendent God can only be recognized and encountered if the other is welcomed in the proximity of the neighbour. Then God exposes himself by calling me to my responsibility, in the face of the stranger, the poor, the widow and the orphan. God is always this nothing of which I speak, but he is this other person whose servant I am and who shows for me the level at which God reveals himself.

4. If we think of the encounter with God like this, we are led to a different way of talking about God from that of the philosophical discourse of transcendence. If God reveals himself in the salvation that I address to others and the homage that I pay them, that must be the situation of the word and the discourse which try to express the ineffable character of this encounter. The transcendence which is then to be expressed is a transcendence of justice, of love, of holiness and mercy. This transcendence 'beyond being' excludes the numinous and terrifying sacred, and calls human beings to a freedom which creates humanity. Any other conception of transcendence, which implies that human beings have access to true life only by escaping from here in the privileged moments of liturgical or mystical exaltation, or by dying, is only a primitive and idolatrous form of transcendence. Theological reflection, too, can only have as its foundation the contemplation of the face of the suffering servant, the face of Christ, the paradigm of the face of the other, the one space where God visits us.

5. Such an anthropology of God, that one can truly call theology of liberation, would show that the historical revelation of the transcendent God in the face of the other disrupts the human order of life and thought. At a point like this we are perpetually tempted, in our life and in our reflection, to re-establish this order by developing more convenient theodicies and theologies. In every possible way we try to interpret on the basis of our customs and our evidence the visit of the God who encounters us. Under the laudable pretext of adapting the Word of revelation to times and cultures, we put this revelation 'in the horizontal', integrating it into a broader and more complex order, a human order, which is given as an evident reference. We then reduce the scandal of the unforeseeable and the unthinkable, the unforgettable and the unhoped-for, in the categories and names of the face of the other.

Thus all discourse about God, analogical discourse which interprets the signs of his presence, and apophatic discourse which stresses his absence, is both justified and disqualified. It is justified, because it is necessary and useful to follow the 'traces' of God along the ways of our life and experience, in the sad wound of his absence. But such discourse is disqualified, in the sense that, like our actions, it fails on the threshold of this separate and silent word which speaks in the face of the other. We then learn that the only mode of being for transcendence is humility, that of the disfigured face of Christ, that of the face of the person who is abandoned, outcast, persecuted, mortal. This humility allows transcendence always to escape all our efforts to put it in order. This indicates that the only way of encountering and thinking of God is to take the side of the one who is humiliated, vanquished, poor and harried. We do not encounter God by having high thoughts or 'states of the soul', but by refusing to enter the existing order and living out an active solidarity with those who, whether beggars or stateless, have nowhere to lay their heads. God is in this alliance with the humility of the humiliated person, who is an absolute disruption. The transcendence of God does not therefore present itself in an absolute of life and thought, but concentrates itself in the gesture which makes me exist for the other. All the rest is still and always less than transcendence.

The person who performs this gesture of homage to the other is no longer rooted in the world and no longer belongs to the world. Leaving their familiar landscapes, forgetting the sweetness of sects and chapels, heretics of all the worlds, such people become God's emigrants. In the luxuriance of human beings and their many savage metamorphoses, they then bear witness to a plural and fraternal humanity.

In this way they arrive at the recognition of which St Paul speaks in his letter to the Colossians (3.15). In the salvation that they direct to the others and the hospitality that they offer them, they part company with the reassuring rumours of common morality, keep away from majority interpretations of the law, and challenge all social consensuses which allow human beings to survive. Always supporters of the other who is outcast, persecuted, mortal, in a history of violence and blood, through division and failings, they begin to exist before God.

Translated by John Bowden

No More Temple, No Place for the Spirit: Tests for the Institutional Church

Isabelle Chareire

The gospel is a paradoxical proclamation of God; God takes our humanity without losing his absolute transcendence in the process. Made present in our history, he leaves a trace which is for ever elusive in the event of the empty tomb. 'God is Spirit, and those who worship him must worship him in spirit and in truth' (John 4.24): neither Mount Gerizim nor Jerusalem have some intrinsic character which makes them adequate places for giving thanks; the criterion of true worship is not a place but pureness of heart. God does not allow himself to be localized; God has no fixed abode. The true temple is the body of the one who was crucified and has risen (John 2.21), who gives the presence of the Spirit to the community of believers: the Spirit which can be discerned but never grasped, as is suggested by the conversation between Jesus and Nicodemus (John 3.8).

The church, the body of which Christ is the head (Col. 1.18), is born in the dynamic of the Spirit of Pentecost: it is charged with bearing witness to this God made visible by the risen Jesus of Nazareth. The Christian community is immediately at the heart of an insurmountable contradiction: proclaiming a Word, performing actions to bear witness to a truth which surpasses them, to bear witness to a God inalienable from human beings, who chooses to reveal himself by human mediations. That is why the church is simultaneously mystical and institutional,[1] and its truth resides in the unity in tension of these two poles. It is a mystical communion with the God whose kingdom it proclaims and the visible witness in history of the eschatological fulfilment. As a public and communal witness the church is institutional, and it is with this institutional reality, in its relationship to the invisible to which it bears witness, that we are concerned here. How can the visible, historic witness, the necessary intermediary in giving an account of the God of Jesus Christ, bear witness to the Inalienable One without giving him a fixed abode?

In order to discuss this question I shall analyse the meaning of a double truth of the church: that it is both instituted and instituting. Then we shall study the articulation of these two poles in the authority of the Word on the one hand and the sacramental dimension on the other.

1. The church, instituted and instituting

An institution is an organized social entity which responds to a legislation, a regulation which is determined and not arbitrary; a stable structure which ensures coherence in social space and duration. It is a constraining point of reference, since it is 'anterior to the individuals who find in it a model for their behaviour and an indication of their role in the group'.[2] P.-A. Liégé distinguishes three institutional spheres in the Christian community:[3] first the Christo-apostolic institution, i.e. the church as instituted by Christ; then the ecclesial institution, a reality which itself institutes. Finally, there is the temporal institution. This comprises the institutional forms corresponding to the tasks undertaken by the church but which do not come under its specific mission (teaching, public aid, health); I shall be leaving aside this third aspect, which is not relevant here.

Is it legitimate, as P.-A. Liégé does, to put that which is instituted entirely on the side of the Christo-apostolic church, and that which institutes exclusively on the side of the ecclesial institution? Or, to ask the question in another way, what does it mean for the church to be instituted or instituting? If the Christo-apostolic institution is defined as 'that part, for ever privileged, of the institution in the Church which engages the faith of the disciples in the very name of the confession of faith',[4] then the canon of scriptures, the service of the continuity of the apostolic mission, the sacraments and the constitution of the particular churches come under what is instituted. The Christo-apostolic institution is certainly 'a gift of the paschal Christ in the Spirit of Pentecost',[5] but this gift is primarily administered by the community of the disciples. The canon of scripture is the most striking example of this interaction: under the guidance of the Spirit the church acts in instituting. And what the article I have quoted assigns to the instituting sphere, for example the *magisterium* as an extension of the canon, seems to me also to be marked by this ambiguity: it is a charismatic inspiration administered by human beings.

It is not for me here to deny the absolutely[6] foundational and fundamental status of the Christo-apostolic sphere, but to stress that God made flesh at once took the risk of delivering himself up to the fragility and the force of human witness. The vigour of the breath of the Spirit and the human fragility which receives it and bears it are indissociable. As a witness instituted by Christ, the church is both attested and attesting. It is attested by Christ as witness, and attests the truth of the God to whom it bears witness. As a guarantor the church makes laws and encloses; it demarcates inner and outer space, develops criteria for belonging, in order to identify, discern, distinguish. The scriptures are the revealed Word, but their canon is determined by the church; the sacraments are effective signs of grace, grace which is at the very source of their institution.

The institutional church is responsible for identifying what gives an authentic account of the Inalienable. How can it cope with this contradiction?

2. The church, witness to the Word of God

The first context of this test is that of revelation: how can the church be witness to a revealed word – which thus has a definitive character – about a God who escapes it?

The church is witness to the Word of God as saving event and revelation. According to Barth, revelation, the Bible, preaching, are the three forms under which the Word of God presents itself.[7] I am going to take up these three forms, shifting the stress on preaching to the church. The Word of God is revelation in the event of the Immanuel, God with us: it is the paschal event which is the basis for the other two forms of the Word of God. Received in faith, the holy scripture is the Word of God to the degree that it 'bears witness to the past revelation and it is God's past revelation in the form of attestation'.[8] The Word of God is ultimately preaching, or the witness of the believing community which has been raised up by the Word of God which it proclaims; the Word of God is at the same time the object and the judge of the church's proclamation.

The authority of the word of God cannot be conceived of outside the dynamic tension between these three poles. In Christianity 'one can never dissociate the authority of the scriptures from that of Christ and the church', writes Claude Geffré,[9] who emphasizes that this authority functions in an original way as compared with the other monotheisms. The authority of the Christian scriptures resides in the authority of their witness, which refers back to the ultimate referent, Christ. Thus this authority is not static, but dynamic. The dynamic of this authority lies in the tension on the one hand between the *magisterium* and the *sensus fidei* on the other hand and between the collective conscience and the individual conscience.[10]

Lumen Gentium stresses that 'the holy People of God shares also in Christ's prophetic office': inspired by the Spirit, the community of the faithful 'from the bishops to the last of the faithful'[11] cannot err in matters of faith. If it is easy to affirm this theoretically, it is more tricky to put it into practice. As Claude Geffré stresses, the dialectic between the *magisterium* and the base is not a simple relationship of theorized practice or applied theory. What is involved here is the regulatory function which all Christians exercise by daily putting into practice their baptism in relation to their faith. The specific implementation of the faith of the church by all the baptized constitutes this faith which they welcome as a gift. As an institutional memory the *magisterium* is not the sole guarantee of the truth of faith; it is realized in the interplay between the institutional expression of the faith and the actualized expression of this faith. On the other hand, if the institution precedes the individuals and determines their behaviour, the institutional constraint makes sense in the church only if it is internalized in specific spiritual experience, but this last has an objective point of reference as its norm (that is the meaning of Rom. 10.9–10). The witness becomes authentic in the confrontation between the communal expression of the faith and the personal expression of the faith.

In this confrontation between the *magisterium* and the *sensus fidei*, what is it that allows this truth to develop? Pascal writes: 'The sole aim of Scripture is charity. All which tends not to the sole end is the type of it. For since there is only one end, all which does not lead to it in express terms is figurative.'[12] The fruits of truth are faith, hope and love – in other words, persistent faithfulness to the Lord, unfailing hope over and above trials, and fulfilment in the performing of the new commandment. The tree needs time to bear its fruits, and the church needs time to discern whether spring will fulfil 'the promise of flowers'. The truth of the reception of the Word of God resides in its fidelity to what has been transmitted: a faithfulness which is more than parroting. The witness born to the ultimate point of reference must be actualized in present history if it is to be effective. This present implementation must be compared with tradition – the canon of the scriptures, the living reading of which constantly gives rise to new interpretations. The text offers resistance at this point: the novelty of the interpretation cannot lead to any questioning of the canon. To affirm the stability of the canon is not to give it a status to which the scriptures have no right in Christianity – which would exclude the interplay with the two other forms of the Word of God – but to state that 'the principle is no part of that of which it is the principle'.[13] To begin with this basic prohibition, which excludes the quest for a canon in the canon, does not lead to a fixed reading. It is part of the sacred riches of the scriptures that this body of scripture, in a historical location, can be constantly actualized. The profound inspiration of scripture is that it is the letter inhabited by the Spirit, but which bears the Spirit. The Spirit without the letter remains mute, but the letter without the Spirit does not exist. The letter is there for the Spirit and not the Spirit for the letter.

3. The church as the 'sacrament of the encounter with God'

'The church, in Christ, is in the nature of sacrament – a sign and instrument, that is, of communion with God and of unity among all men.'[14] This quotation from *Lumen Gentium* introduces us to the second type of test that the Christian community must undergo. How can it bear witness to the truth of the encounter of humanity with God while affirming the absolute freedom of its divine partner?

In the sacraments, too, the church is eminently instituted and instituting. In my analysis of this double reality of the sacramental church I owe much to the work of L.-M. Chauvet.[15] The sacraments are the most institutional ecclesial mediation, since in them the church is completely involved as such. So the church has complete control over their performance, 'their substance being saved'. This formula of the Council of Trent allows us to identify the paradox of the sacraments. Affirming that it receives the sacraments from Jesus Christ, the church recognizes that it is not master of them: 'nothing is in total more regulated by it than what it recognizes as escaping its control'.[16] When the church says that the sacraments which it administers were instituted by Christ, it recognizes that it is dependent on the Lord in the very act of the sacrament, and it affirms that it does not have the power to invent this action which it welcomes as a grace, as an institution which precedes it.

In recognizing that the institution of the sacraments is not part of it, the church gives specific expression to the otherness of God; the Christian tension with the beyond is not the imaginary projection of the divinized human being, but the desire of a subject which lets go of itself to rise towards the radically other. The basic prohibition, which amounts to the acceptance that one receives oneself absolutely from an other, gives structure to the Christian identity, just as it is the identity of the human subject. The radical otherness of God is embodied in some way in the sacramental reality. Its elusiveness makes itself flesh to indicate that it relates to a divine objectivity.

We have just seen how L.-M. Chauvet's analysis allows us to think of the paradoxical character of the sacraments received by the church as a gift. However, the sacraments are not only instituted but also instituting: they give an identity.[17] How do we affirm that the sacraments are events of grace? To avoid the objectivist impasse or excessive subjectivism, Vatican II opens up a middle way[18] and affirms simultaneously:

– the salvation given by God does not depend on the sacraments; these reveal the grace that is already present in human life. As such, they are acts of recognition by the human being towards God;

– God is the operative subject of the sacraments; in this sense the sacrament is constitutive of the Christian life which, in turn, is a sweet-smelling perfume, thanksgiving to God.

Here we have to think these two truths simultaneously: the sacraments are both revelatory and operative; in other words, the freedom of grace and its efficacious manifestation in the sacraments. The ritual language and symbolic efficacy of the rites allow L.-M. Chauvet to think of the sacraments as 'operative symbolic expressions'. The sacraments act as revealers, i.e. symbolically and not magically. The sacraments reveal by being operative: to perform a ritual act, to speak a word ('I promise you, I forgive you') is to bring about a truth.

Of course all this does not exhaust the elusive nature of the character of grace, but says that it is 'for us' and not that it is 'in itself' or for God, since that radically escapes us. Thus, to take up Chauvet's image, the sacrament is an event of grace, not as a treasure buried in a field, but as that which comes to give us new direction, to convert the baptized so that they are open to the desire of the absolutely Other. The objective reality of the sacramental act is aimed at showing the elusiveness of grace – not to alienate it from subjectivity. It is a manifestation which is not a simple instrumentation, but is an event in itself, and at the same time a manifestation which has no power over that which it expresses.

Conclusion

The *sensus fidei* and the *magisterium* interact in tension to produce the truth of the witness. The sacrament oscillates between the inalienability of the gift received and its institutional administration on the one hand and the objectivity of the gift to which it bears witness and the subjectivity of the person involved in it in the other.

In his book *Provisional Churches*,[19] Christian Duquoc writes that it is in the dialectical tension between the provisional and the symbolic that the churches bear witness to the Ultimate. It seems to me that the enquiry I have just carried out fits into this dynamic. The truth of the institutional reality of the church lies in its historical dimension: as history it is what happens in eschatological expectation; but as history it is also the symbolic place in which this expectation makes its mark. To signify the One to whom it bears witness the church must be both closed and open: closed, to signify concretely the otherness of the One from whom it receives itself; open, to escape any seizure of the absolute. It is in maintaining these two poles that the truth of its witness rises 'until the day dawns and the morning star rises in (our) hearts' (II Peter 1.19).

Translated by John Bowden

Notes

1. Cf. *Lumen Gentium* 8.
2. Y. Congar, quoted by P.-A. Liégé, 'Place à l'institution dans l'Eglise. Legitimations doctrinales', in *L'Eglise: institution et foi*, Brussels 1979, 175f.
3. Ibid.
4. Ibid., 178.
5. Ibid.
6. 'Absolutely': in a perfect way, finished, because it is the work of the Absolute himself.
7. Cf. Karl Barth, *Church Dogmatics* I.1, Edinburgh ²1975, 111.
8. Ibid.
9. 'Autorité des Ecritures et autonomie de la conscience', *Le Supplément* 155, December 1985, 67.
10. Here I shall examine the internal aspect of this test, but there is also an external aspect: in its faith the church denotes God revealing himself in the particular event of the crucified Jesus, whose resurrection bears witness to his Lordship. So Jesus is affirmed as universal saviour and revealer of the true face of God. However, the Spirit bears witness to the elusiveness of God. What does that mean for a positive recognition of other religions?
11. *Lumen Gentium* 12 quotes St Augustine here!
12. Pascal, *Pensées* 669, Everyman edition, London 1908, p. 188. For this question see the illuminating article by A. Delzant, 'Révélation, canon, interprétations', *Lumière et vie* 171, January–March 1985.
13. Delzant, 'Révélation, canon, interprétations'.
14. *Lumen Gentium* 1.

15. L.-M. Chauvet, *Symbole et sacrement: une relecture sacramentelle de l'existence chrétienne*, Paris 1987.

16. Ibid., 389.

17. I stress that the word instituting is used here in a different sense from that in P.-A. Liégé: not what establishes an institution, but what establishes the identity of the subject.

18. Ibid., 423.

19. C. Duquoc, *Provisional Churches*, London 1986. The multiplicity of churches is read as an opportunity to indicate better that to which they bear witness: 'The more they accept the provisional character of their forms, their structures and their strategies, the closer they come to the kingdom and the better they bear witness to it' (97). By attaching weight to the provisional character of this world, the symbolism also expresses its incompleteness, a tension with that which is still to come.

'We Proclaim a Crucified Messiah'

José-Ignacio González-Faus SJ

'Where is God? I don't know.
I haven't seen that gentleman.
He must be having breakfast
at the master's table' (Atahualpa Yupanki).

'Where is God? I'll tell you. You and I have killed him. We are all his murderers' (Nietzsche).

'Where have you hidden yourself,
Beloved, and left me groaning?' (St John of the Cross).

'As with a deadly wound in my body,
my adversaries taunt me,
while they say to me continually, "Where is your God?"' (Psalm 42)

'The Lord has done great things for us; we are glad' (Psalm 126)

An impressive range of human experience could be listed which has crystallized in the tortured question, 'Where is God?' or in the startled conclusion (almost always in the past): 'God has been here.' These experiences can be individual, collective or historical.

Precisely because of the recurrent nature of these experiences, we may add that there exists in the Christian tradition a general structure for answering the question about God's hiddenness. This structure contains at least these three elements: (*a*) the inherent nature of God (He is a 'hidden God'), (*b*) the inherent difficulty of history (God is like the summit of a mountain which disappears when we start walking towards it), and (*c*) human sin (God is not here because 'we ourselves' have expelled him, as Nietzsche said).

This framework, however, precisely because it is valid for *all* answers, is too general when the questions become specific. The question I have been given is very specific: where is God precisely when all the messianic hopes (political, social or ecclesiastical) in which many people in our modern time thought they could find him are breaking down? The answer to this question is not obvious. It has to be looked for afresh, through a 'dark night' like the one John of the Cross went through, 'with no other light or guide but the one burning in my heart'.

I. The dark night of history

For this search I shall consider a series of historical experiences. The first two are normative for Christians. The others are our own, from today. Perhaps they can be read in the light of the earlier ones.

Normative experiences

1. The history of Israel

The experience of the Jewish people is an inescapable paradigm. All believers are in agreement that in the departure from Egypt there took place an authentic 'revelation' and an authentic experience of God. Egypt was 'the house of slavery'. (But it is important to note in passing that this is only a judgment of faith. In the judgment of history, Egypt was instead 'an advanced civilization', and one more example of the effectiveness of force. It functioned as a 'dictatorship'. Today all that is left is the memory of its astonishing achievements. The memory of the blood with which they were constructed long ago dissolved in the waters of the Nile. We will not find it in the history books, nor in the British Museum or the Cairo Museum.)

But what interests us now is this other detail: the people who believed they had found God because they left Egypt don't seem to find him by really reaching the promised land. The departure from Egypt is almost disappointing when we analyse its results. The biblical model suggests a range of reasons for this disappointment with the promised land:

(*a*) *The inherent density of reality*. The promised land was not magic. It did not 'flow with milk and honey', as the people had naively hoped.

(*b*) *The novelty of history*. The people established in Canaan would have to face new problems which they had not known during slavery in Egypt. They had no guarantees that they would give these problems the answer which leads to God.

(*c*) *The temptation of the surrounding world*. God's freedom has a lot to do with gratuitousness and therefore with a lack of pretentiousness. And the human thirst for power was to lead Israel to prefer 'to have a king like the other nations', in order to achieve, like them, a passing splendour.

(*d*) This may be the source of *the inherent sin of the Chosen One*. Israel was to establish in its new land many types of oppression similar to those it had suffered in Egypt. In spite of so many inspired voices ('Remember that you too were a stranger in Egypt'), Israel preferred to reject its own *memoria passionis*. It is striking to see how this pattern is being reproduced today in the violence of the Israeli state.

And the unkindest cut: this Old Testament pattern, far from being cancelled, was to be carried to an extreme by the coming of the Messiah.

2. The history of Jesus
In the case of Jesus there is nothing to compare with what in Israel had been 'the sin of the Chosen One'. In his messianic temptations Jesus was to behave differently from the people of the Old Testament. But this fact does not break the pattern we have just noticed; instead it confirms it.

Jesus too, when he started out, was familiar with the sensation that 'the kingdom of God is at hand' (cf. Mark 1.15; Matt. 12.28; Luke 10.9) or that the Son from on high has visited and redeemed his people to give light to those who live in the shadows of death and to guide our feet into the ways of peace (cf. Luke 1.68–79). But Jesus ends his life recognizing that the kingdom of God 'is not of this world' – since God is not prepared to defend it by force (cf. John 18.36) – and gasping out the same question about abandonment by God (Mark 15.34). I repeat, Jesus did not fall into messianic temptations, nor did he allow the messianic cause to be measured by 'sabbaths' which force human beings to serve them. This did not prevent, but rather encouraged the dense web of interests implanted in history and contrary to any true messianism to see him as a real threat (cf. John 11.47ff). As a result Jesus was denounced, declared a friend of sinners, a blasphemer, a person who led the people astray.

Despite the variations the Old Testament pattern persists: God, who makes himself present at the moment of 'leaving Egypt' seems to disappear at the moment of 'reaching the kingdom'. Christian faith starts from this double experience, that of the Old Testament and that of Jesus. It is not just prior to it. That is why faith is formulated in that desperate way: 'We preach a crucified Messiah' (I Cor. 1.23).

Present-day experiences

1. The Nicaraguan pattern
On few occasions in history has a group of Christians felt more intensely the suspicion of witnessing a 'passover of God' than the Christians of Nicaragua in 1979. This suspicion was not simply one more case of a revolution lucky enough to win. No archive of the civilized world has a

record of all the lives offered, the bodies given up and the blood shed to give life. But, for a moment, they made an impact on our memory when in the Nicaragua of 1979 they sang the lines: 'On every road, on every path and track, I discern, Christ Jesus, the light of your truth' (Sanctus of the Nicaraguan Mass).

Only twelve years later, all that is left is the question, 'Where is that God who seemed to pass through the history of Nicaragua?' So far the two patterns run in parallel.

In the answer to this question we will keep coming across individual features and differences of analysis. I believe that in the case of Nicaragua, as in that of Israel, we have to speak of a series of grave sins of the Sandinista leaders. This does not prevent us from recognizing at the same time the fact of the sentence of death pronounced by the empire, which was carried out with total impunity, with the mining of harbours, the imposition of embargoes, contempt for the verdict of international courts like that of The Hague and the funding of an entire mercenary army. Nor does it prevent our recognizing also the way the Nicaraguan project was depicted as the embodiment of evil by those who have absolute control of all the information on the planet.

Now that the Sandinista movement has been overthrown, Nicaragua has ceased to be newsworthy, although its situation has not improved at all and it endures the same sufferings as before. But the Empire's plan was not about helping Nicaragua or democracy, but about avoiding at all costs 'the threat of a good example'. To achieve this, even more than defeating it, it was necessary to force it to pervert itself. At the same time, the high priests of the system persuaded public opinion to shout 'Crucify them!' (cf. Matt. 27.20ff.). Once this aim was achieved, the mere absence of information would work on us in terms of the saying, 'No news is good news', even though everything continued in as bad a state as before.

2. Other examples

It would be easy to mention other failed revolutions, even without considering the failure in Eastern Europe (since that was an example of 'messianism against God'). Guatemala, Mexico and Cuba have also passed through 'exodus' situations. The Guatemalan revolution (the most moderate, whose agrarian reform law declared that it sought to 'develop the capitalist agricultural economy') was destroyed in 1954 by the United States' senseless invasion.[1] Ever since Guatemala has been undergoing a long crucifixion, with one of the highest rates of injustice and violence on the planet, but, curiously, receives very little attention. The Mexican revolution seems to have collapsed of its own accord, through the internal decay of the PRI, which, like Israel's monarchy, seemed necessary in order to perpetuate itself in power. The current agony of Cuba tends to provoke much more passionate judgments since, despite our appeals to critical reason, the 'enlightened' world continues to think in a 'fundamentalist' way where it detects a threat to its security. In my modest opinion, Cuba has regained much of its dignity (in relation to the United States), and part of its independence (by trying to free itself from dependence on sugar). But (*a*) it was forced to throw itself unconditionally into the arms of the Soviet Union, and (*b*) after the first level of material liberation (food, health and education, in which for a moment Cuba seemed to be Latin America's promised land) it too became corrupt and was unable to distribute the word and freedom as it had previously distributed bread.

Whatever our analysis of these processes, they are mentioned here, not to give a detailed explanation, but to recall the situations of slavery which preceded them, when Batista's Cuba was a North American brothel, with more prostitutes than productive workers, and in Mexico the landowners' horses ate many times better than their workers. To forget these details would contribute to increasing the eclipse of God we are trying to study, and would make us liable to the psalmist's ancient curse: 'May my tongue cleave to the roof of my mouth if I forget you.'

3. The imperial pattern
Instead of a series of descriptions, it may be more interesting to consider a final historical pattern, in this case the victorious pattern of the empires. Successive governments of the United States have embarked on a cruel and exaggerated arms race – God alone knows whether from fear or arrogance. The dilemma whether to use the threat of military force or financial corruption has always been a constant in all its historical actions. No so long ago the Iraqi tyrant thought in his madness – fostered by the Empire – that he could behave in an imperial manner with his tyrant neighbours. He was deceived by an apparently connivent silence about the consequences of an invasion of Kuwait. Europe was shocked, but was only too anxious to be shocked, by the scale of the Iraqi threat: an army which this time did deserve the pejorative label 'Third World' was presented to world opinion as 'the fourth largest on earth'. In this context it was easy to brandish arguments about our own 'moral stature' and the need for 'an exemplary punishment', with the theoretical excuse of the need to define a peace which not even the 'exemplary' punishment of Hiroshima and Nagasaki had succeeded in

guaranteeing, but with the practical objective of preserving what Noam Chomsky calls 'the fifth freedom'. And if anyone doesn't share this analysis, they may simply ponder the words of President W. H. Taft in 1912: 'The whole of the hemisphere will be ours in fact, just as, by virtue of our racial superiority, it is already ours morally.' Therefore US foreign policy 'in no way excludes active intervention to guarantee our goods and our capitalists facilities for profitable investments'.[2]

I am not making these remarks in order to annoy anyone, but I think it necessary to make them because, curiously, in the whole history of the empires the question of where God is has never been raised. God has been constantly invoked, and President Bush takes His Holy Name in the same forensic tone with which the Jews appealed to God at the foot of Jesus' cross. In the victorious pattern the question of God's absence doesn't seem to arise, whatever the means with which the victory was achieved: the final victory justifies them.

All these elements put back on the table (now with more detail) the difficult question, 'Where is God?'

II. With no other light or guide than that which burned in my heart

More on biblical paradigms

The famous vision in Chapter 7 of the book of Daniel, one of the oldest theologies of history, may provide some elements of an answer. Let us recall the vision and its oppositions.

Out of the stormy sea come 'four beasts'. From the calm heavens there appears 'something like a human figure' (v. 13). The beasts may have 'feet like a man' (v. 4), wings (v. 6) and above all teeth (vv. 5, 7: 'great iron teeth [which] devoured and broke in pieces'). The human figure merges into a collective, 'the saints of the Most High' (v. 18). Finally the beasts stand for the 'four kings who shall arise' (v. 17) in the history familiar to the seer, references to the empires of Babylon, the Medes, the Persians and Alexander. The son of man is the real owner of the power the beasts have seized (v. 14), but the saints have been left in the power of the beasts for an indeterminate and incalculable time ('a time, two times and half a time', v. 25).

This condensed summary is enough for us to attempt a translation of the allegory for us:

Out of the confusion of history come the empires. If we transpose the allegory to Western history the four empires could be the Roman empire, the Spanish empire, the British empire and the United States empire. The empires are contrary to God's will for history; they are both cruel and effective. They are invincible, but have distorted human features, which make them look more like beasts. But the empires are subjected to the judgment of the 'Ancient of Days' (v. 9), and their power is never eternal, though it may appear so to the diminutive scale of each individual. The power of God is on the side of the victims. The prophet knows this, not because he has been told when this shift of power will be seen, but because he has seen that the victims had human shapes (the ambiguity of the expression 'son of man', which can mean both a disreputable appearance and transcendent dignity) and as such had been presented to the Ancient (v. 13).

In conclusion: history remains subject to this painful ambiguity in which we see on the one hand the victory of injustice, but on the other can just make out the logic of the just and defeated. And God does not appear in history as intervening in it to remove this ambiguity, but because the ambiguity remains intact: only God can uphold the logic of those 'without logic'.

This ambiguity, according to the Fourth Gospel, only disappears with the arrival of the Advocate of the weak, whose mission is to show that there is sin, justice and judgment (John 16.8), and show where each of these is. Sin is not believing in Jesus (John 16.9), shown by placing the values of security, efficiency and immediate victory above the values of the dignity of the children of God. Justice is 'going to the Father', though this cannot yet be seen – it is Jesus' axiology and not that of the world (16.10). Judgment is the fact that 'the Structural Principle of this world has been exposed' (16.11) by the number of innocent victims it demands, who all now crowd together and win back a body in Jesus, the Divine Victim.

'You cannot serve God and money' (Matt. 6.24)

If this scriptural vision is correct, we must suspect that the question where God is can only be asked when we accept in advance being judged by God. I am well aware that 'being judged by God' sounds unacceptable to modern people who – in their radical despair – feel, on the contrary, that they are in a position to summon God to judgment. It is therefore necessary to explain that 'letting oneself be judged by God' means no more than deciding to accept the truth about oneself, taking the victims as the criterion of this truth about ourselves.

In order to go forward, therefore, we need to make a critique of our historical progress from the point of view of its victims. Put another way, it means confronting 'the spirit of progress' with the Holy Spirit.[3]

This proposal does not imply any conservative attack on the category of progress as such, which is one of the most theologal categories in our language. It does imply, however, repentance for this particular form of progress, for this particular world. Above all, it implies a rethinking of the messianic claims of our technological progress.

I stress the point about messianism because I took the failure of historical messianisms as the starting point for our discussion. They have been left with no alternative than to produce victims in their turn if they want to be effective in the stormy sea of history (and so they end up turning into new 'beasts' from Daniel's vision), or to be inevitably crushed like Jesus if they refuse to be inhuman. Another reason is that in this context the sense of the failure of historical forms of messianism could encourage new messianic claims for technological progress, whose results are tangible, spectacular and highly comfortable. But if we were to look for God in this only form of messianism which seems successful, we would be forgetting the inescapable Christian qualification on any revelation of God, the *memoria passionis*. The messianism of progress would seek to find God through its mere practical efficiency, without thought for the human blood shed to achieve this efficiency, just as the Pharisees at the foot of the cross appealed to God in the satisfaction of their victory. But that god was not the God who revealed himself in Jesus.

And so: human progress or 'blood for oil'?

If this is the situation, it will be clear why, if we are to find God in the First World, we cannot start just from the present, but from the past. We have to confess the sin of the historical progress whose real beneficiaries we are, or perform a theological interpretation of 'the dialectic of the Enlightenment': not that this proposal implies an attack on the category of 'enlightenment' as such, which is absolutely irreplaceable (even in theology), but it does presuppose an examination of what we regard as enlightenment.

So, the dialectic, or the sin of our progress, is based on the fact that it has built its astonishing efficiency on evil, on a one-dimensional reduction, on plunder and deceit.

The evil was in the primary accumulation, in the gold and silver which came from Latin America to Europe (and were well and industriously employed in Central Europe and frittered away in Spain, of course, though that makes no difference to the evil of their acquisition). It was in the trade in African slaves (which provided both labour for the colonies and capital for the metropolitan countries), and in the brutal extortion of raw materials in a commerce which was never free or equitable. Where would historical progress have got to without this threefold evil?

Human multidimensionality (so difficult to integrate) has been reduced to a pure 'instrumental reason' which has burned up countless human elements and values in a 'bonfire of the vanities' in which the only thing that counts is production for its sake. Production is no longer for human needs (which for the most part remain unsatisfied in the era of the greatest productivity ever seen), but 'human beings are for production' (cf. Mark 2.27).[4]

The plundering of the planet has turned the necessary communion of human beings with nature into a massacre of nature. It is true that we are more aware of this today, but I don't know whether this is because of a genuine rediscovery of kinship with nature or from fear of its unexpected revenge. But it is not certain that we can reverse the massacre.

The deceit lies in the presentation of all this distorted, monstrous progress as the true and only possible progress, and justifying its evils by its dazzling successes and dulling our suspicions by intoxicating us with its addictions.[5]

Is our sense of the death of God fulfilling that judgment on the 'impiety and injustice of men who make God's truth a prisoner by their injustice' (Rom 1.18)? The question can have more radical or more moderate answers, but the First World cannot avoid it because, in a curious way, it is exclusively our question. In Latin America or India other questions arise which may be more agonizing, but not this one. There God is not felt to be absent.

And yet to accept the question may turn out to be very difficult for us, for two reasons, not only because repentance may cost us very dear, but also because, now above all, with so many of our problems solved, we can be more aware than others of the dignity of the person, of human rights, and the evil of any production of victims. And this awareness also enables us to condemn all those who, as a result of the conditions in which we perhaps force them to live, have still to reach it.

At all events, perhaps the beginning of a response is to be found in the following lines of Bishop Casaldáliga's, in which the question which underlies this article also appears, but in modified form:

These poor women of the land
who die giving life
in a world which kills them!
This uninhabitable house
which was the house of your Son!
Where are we, you and we, our Father?

The question which, confronted with this bloody history, cries out, 'Where is God?', can only begin to be answered if it turns into another question which includes the questioner: 'Where are we, you and we?' Of course we are talking now of general, cultural historical judgments rather than particular cases, but our specific experience in many particular situations is to find ourselves utterly impotent.

III 'I have seen the Lord' (John 20.18)

Only when the question has been modified in this way can we suggest some elements of an answer. The Christian concept of God brings at least three important differences from the 'general idea of God'. First there are the essential qualifications of the kingdom and the cross, which have been referred to in various ways in the previous sections. Then there is the idea of the Trinity, which will be the focus of the rest of the discussion. Both Moltmann and Kitamori remarked some years ago on the extent to which the idea of the Trinity forces us to use dialectical (or apparently contradictory) language about God. God is not only the One and the Plural, but also the Impassible who can suffer and the Inaccessible who can be found.[6]

It is striking that, whereas the Trinity plays little part in the faith of most Christians, it has been a decisive element in the theologal experience of almost all the mystics. The mystics, with their simultaneous appeals to 'nothingness', 'knowing nothing', 'fusion' and 'embrace', enable us to see that God is primarily the inaccessible Origin, but, because he is also the Principle of self-communication and rediscovery of self, he can also be unexpectedly recognized by us and be a Power of recognition in us. In the part of our history which we discussed earlier, God is to be discovered in those who are crucified, through commitment to them, and he can be discovered thanks to that history's unswerving 'aspiration' to be freed from frustration (cf. 8.19): no one can call a victim of that history a 'child of God' except in the Spirit (cf. I Cor 12.3). But through, and only through, both mediations – that of committed love and that of aspiring hope – the Inaccessible Origin seems to come out to meet human beings and can be called in faith *Abba*, Father. This illustrates what John of Salisbury wrote long ago in the twelfth century, referring to the trinitarian debates around Gilbert de la Porrée, that, since language is designed only for our purposes, in theology we can only talk adequately about faith, hope and charity (which are 'our' achievement thanks to God). The rest is beyond all knowledge.[7]

Against this background the question 'Where is God?' also acquires an important modification. In one sense, we can never say where God is. We can often say where the victims are with whom he identifies in the Crucified One, despite the blindness of our hearts. But perhaps the most important question is where the Spirit of God is. It is important above all for the First World, which is largely the offspring of the Western theological tradition, in which the Holy Spirit is the great absentee. This absence gives us food for thought, since human beings have no other way of rediscovering God than rediscovering his Spirit.

I will finish with the words of a Spanish hymn which I have talked about before. Its very title ('Little Explanations') contains a dash of innocent irony because, with the discretion of a person who doesn't stop to meddle, it stays in the centre of our question and gives what may be the decisive part of the answer. The hymn has a standard pattern which recurs in each verse, and so there is no need to quote them all. The pattern lists a number of 'secular' situations: 'When someone has nothing and still shares, when a poor person is thirsty and gives us water, when someone creates peace where there is war, when we love the intuitions of the simple . . .' But the conclusion of each verse does not say that when this happens the world is changed and the messianic promise fulfilled, but, much more discreetly, comments: 'God himself is there in our own journey'. It is 'our own' journey, not some escape route he has provided. And it is God himself, and not some information – however authoritative – about him. In my opinion this idea contains one of the most authentic experiences of the Spirit. Bishop Casaldáliga has commented on this too in these other lines, which share a starting point with us, the certainty of our powerlessness to achieve that *metanoia* I called for in the previous section:

> I don't know if I could live with the poor
> if I didn't find God in their rags;
> if God was not there like a fire,
> burning my egoism slowly.

I must finish. And I want to do so myself with a – double and important – 'little explanation'.

(a) Karl Rahner said that the Christian of the twenty-first century will be a mystic or not a Christian. He was certainly right. Nevertheless, the word 'mysticism' is full of dangers, because it opens the door to spiritualism, evasions and other alienated forms of religion which, from far away on their supposed peaks, in the end do deals with the injustice of history. The Western Enlightenment tradition did well to be suspicious (even before Marx) of such mysticisms. Today, however, in the face of the Calvary of all messianic hopes, it seems that this escapist temptation is trying to reconquer what little religion will be left in the future in the West. I have tried in this article to warn against this pseudo-mysticism, and point out the path to a true, gospel mystical experience. Now, in conclusion, another warning is needed.

(b) Truth (Urs van Balthasar used to say) is symphonic. What I have said here is just the particular part of one instrument, which I was asked to play. Not all the absence of God in the First World is connected with our more than possible historical sin. There is a great variety of individual paths within this area, but they are independent of it. There are histories of personal dark nights, of cultural 'changes of spots', very difficult trials of various types. They are histories which would require a different hermeneutical key, but they are not what I was asked to discuss.

Translated by Francis McDonagh

Notes

1. Nine years later Dwight Eisenhower reached for the obligatory justification: 'We had to get rid of a *Communist* government which had taken power' (see Eduardo Galeano, *The Open Veins of Latin America*, New York, 1973.).

2. Galeano, *Open Veins* (n.l). Also N. Chomsky, *Turning the Tide*, Boston 1985. I would like to note explicitly that Chomsky is as North American as George Bush (just as Las Casas was as Spanish as Pizarro). My point is that nothing I say is intended as an attack on any people. Oppression has no nationality and it is therefore wrong to use patriotism to undermine accusations of oppression.

3. There is a similar attempt, with more attention to economic issues, in M. D. Meek, 'Gott und die Ökonomie des Heiligen Geistes', *Evangelische Theologie* 40, 1980, 40–58.

4. There is no need to recall that almost 1000 million inhabitants of the planet live in a situation of total poverty and hunger, and two-thirds in a situation of want, that tens of thousands of people die every day of hunger, and that 'the military expenditure of all the countries of the world combined amounts to around two million US dollars *every minute*' (R. Habito, *Liberación total*, Madrid 1990, 76–7).

5. Theology has often been an accomplice in this deceit, having been practised by a

church which shared in the rich world's profits, and provided justifications for many evils, including the slave trade. As a result the church today cannot exclusively accuse the world and present itself as a model of fidelity to God, claiming that the root of the problem is solely in the world's atheism. In this context it is better to listen to the profound words of Bishop Pedro Casaldáliga: 'The camel which cannot pass through the eye of a needle gets into any cathedral.' In order to do a theology of liberation we perhaps first have to carry out a 'liberation of theology' (Juan Luis Segundo).

6. Irenaeus of Lyons sometimes formulates this contradiction by speaking of God 'in terms of magnitude' (*secundum magnitudinem*) and 'in terms of love' (*secundum dilectionem*) (cf. *Adv. Haer.* IV, 20, 1). St Augustine has this well-known passage: 'Never new, never old, but making all things new; always active, always still; gathering in and not in want; wanting when you lack nothing. You love, but do not burn, quest and are carefree, repent and do not grieve . . . What does a person say when he says something about you? And woe to those who say nothing about you since those who have much to say are dumb' (*Nonquam novus, nunquam vetus, innovans omnia; semper agens, semper quietus; colligens et non egens; quaerens cum nihil desit tibi. Amas nec aestuas, zelas et securus es, penitet Te et non doles . . . Quid dicit aliquis cum de Te dicit? Et vae tacentibus de Te, quoniam loquaces muti sunt* [*Conf.* I, 4, 4]).

7. '*Nec mirum si de eis nequaquam digne loquimur, cum propriis ad hoc sermonibus careamus . . . Sermones enim instituti sunt ea significare quae continentur in mente. Sed theologica dumtaxat fide, spe et caritate in mente sunt, alias autem, sicut apostolus ait, superant omnem sensum*' (*Historia Pontificalis*, Oxford 1986, 36).

God Sings in the Night: Ambiguity as an Invitation to Believe

Richard G. Cote OMI

Ambiguity is a phenomenon with which we are all familiar. If we think about it at all, it probably appears to us as something rather unsettling, unpleasant, perhaps even threatening. The experience of ambiguity, especially as it impinges upon those vital areas of our Christian life and identity, is not something we welcome, nor are we inclined to see it as a positive element in our life of faith.

Although there is much ambiguity in our modern secular world today, here I want to focus on that peculiar ambiguity which attaches itself to Christian faith. I will argue that ambiguity is not hostile or inimical to faith, but on the contrary is an integral dimension of faith itself, an abiding and necessary summons to believe, and that to have lost this important ability to hear God sing in the night is to have lost a singular opportunity to possess our faith in a deeper and more vital way.

To say that ambiguity is very much part of Christian existence is a theological and pastoral understatement. Not only do we experience ambiguity at certain awkward moments, as when we have to make difficult moral decisions or on those special occasions when we place ourselves in a deliberate posture of Christian discernment. Ambiguity exists at very heart of our life of faith. Indeed faith never yields that kind of certainty which would eliminate all ambiguity and doubt in the believer's consciousness and lived experience.

On this score, the Council of Trent was very explicit: 'No one can know with the certainty of faith that he has obtained the grace of God' (Denzinger, 802). Nor do we know for sure that our sins have indeed been forgiven by God, or that we will in fact persevere to the end and be saved (Denzinger 823, 806). In more recent times, Karl Rahner has shown in what sense the Reformation formula *Simul justus et peccator* (justified and sinner at the same time), when properly understood, is in accordance with Catholic teaching and theology.[1]

In a seminal and truly remarkable study in *Concilium* some years ago, Johannes Metz showed how it is no longer possible to make a clear-cut distinction between belief and unbelief in the actual life of a Christian, that belief and unbelief are real conflicting elements within the activity of believing itself.[2]

The failure to recognize or appreciate this theological truth, I am convinced, has contributed to a certain misguided fundamentalism within the church and to the unwarranted alienation of many believers who now find themselves on the so-called periphery or margin of the church. It will be my contention that the church's intolerance of ambiguity is part of the problem, and that ambiguity cannot be eliminated from the mysterious ways God 'seduces' and lovingly draws us to himself.

Intolerance of ambiguity in Western culture

In our Western culture, 'ambiguity' has long been a pejorative term, something to be eliminated if at all possible. This reflects the general bias in our civilization which, from classical Greek times, put so much confidence in reason and gave such pride of place to the unbroken quest for clarity, precision, exactness and certainty. In such a cultural context, ambiguity could only be regarded as an *enfant terrible*, a temporary annoyance that was to be eliminated as quickly as the rules of sound logic would permit. It represented a failure in the reasoning process and was generally attributed to either excessive brevity, to a deliberate attempt to distort the truth, or just simply to faulty logic.

Of course there has always been a significant minority of individuals in our cultural history who looked more kindly on ambiguity – indeed who seem to have actually thrived on it. I am referring of course to the artists, the poets and the mystics. For them, ambiguity was often the very focus of their creative talents and insights. One need only think of the multiplicity of meanings and hence the ambiguity in a work like Dante's *Divina comedia*, or Shakespeare's *Hamlet*, a play and a character which have both become synonymous with ambiguity. The same is true of visual or aesthetic ambiguity, as in Leonardo's 'Mona Lisa' or Vermeer's 'An Artist in His Studio'.

And the great mystics in our Western culture, too, those who had a truly 'close encounter' with God, with the Holy One, invariably speak of this experience as most ambiguous – something at once 'terrifying' yet 'fascinating' beyond compare. Were we to excise all the ambiguities in the works of John of the Cross, Teresa of Avila, Meister Eckhart, or Ruysbroec, for example, there would be little or nothing left of their mystical experiences.

In philosophy, the genuine acceptance of ambiguity came only in the twentieth century. Earlier thinkers, like Russell, Wittgenstein in his *Tractatus*, and Husserl, tried to overcome ambiguity and leave it behind. The later Wittgenstein, Merleau-Ponty, and the existentialists like Sartre and Simone de Beauvoir, accept ambiguity and make it the basis of their philosophies.

But it was modern psychology and the practitioners of psychoanalysis especially that really brought home to us the fact that ambiguity is an inescapable dimension of being human. Not only did Carl Jung perceive ambiguity at the heart of the human psyche – what he called the *animus* and the *anima* – but, more significantly, he saw it as a necessary precondition for any real growth and development. The point is well made in the following passage:

> Life itself flows from springs both clear and muddy. Hence all excessive 'purity' lacks vitality. A constant striving for clarity and differentiation means a proportionate loss of vital intensity precisely because the muddy elements are excluded. Every renewal of all life needs the muddy as well as the clear.[3]

The psychology of intolerance

It was only forty years ago that psychologists began studying the question of ambiguity directly and why it is that some people have more difficulty than others in coping with ambiguous situations. In psychological terms, intolerance of ambiguity is the tendency to perceive (or interpret) ambiguous situations as sources of threat. They define an ambiguous situation as one that is unclear because of a lack of meaningful cues.

Since the early 1950s, many studies of intolerance of ambiguity have been conducted by means of questionnaires, interviews, projective tests, systematic observation and experimental research. The focus of most of this research has been to determine how intolerance of ambiguity relates to other personality traits. The research findings have shown – indeed have shown quite convincingly – that people who are intolerant of ambiguity are more than likely to evince one or more of the following traits: low self-esteem, rigidity in thinking, close-mindedness, dogmatism, anxiety, strong ethnocentrism, religious fundamentalism, conformity, prejudice and low creativity.

I am suggesting here that intolerance of ambiguity does have implications for the church and the way one's affiliation to the church is perceived and reckoned. Throughout history the on-going debate about who belongs to the church and the criteria against which Christian identification is measured have always been conditioned by the degree of intolerance of ambiguity that prevails in the church at any given time. Thus it comes as no surprise that as early as the fourth century, Saint Augustine acknowledged the ambiguity of church membership when he wrote: 'Some seem to be inside [the church], who are in fact outside, while others seem to be outside who are in fact inside.'[4]

Ambiguity is nothing new in the history of the church, and our experience of it is neither unique nor unprecedented. There are many ambiguities in church life today, many different ways of interpreting certain passages of Scripture, many differing theological viewpoints, and many conflicting views about the proper lifestyle of Christian. There are also many believers today who are living in a real limbo of ecclesiastical ambiguity: the divorced and remarried, the gay and lesbian members of the Christian community, those whose conscience compels them to use artificial means of birth control, those who have come out in favor of the PRO-CHOICE movement, or the feminists in a church that is still male-dominated. What we need, therefore, and what I am suggesting, is a theology of ambiguity.

The God of biblical revelation

The God of Abraham, Isaac and Jacob reveals himself, but always with an essential and ambiguous reserve: as the one who is far and yet near, who is unapproachable and yet who beckons us to come closer, who is intangible and yet can be violated. He reveals himself in history and yet always seems to be receding from it.

In the biblical account of salvation history, the free, unsolicited advances that God is for ever making on our behalf are always steeped in profound ambiguity. At times he appears as wonderful (in the sense of performing wonders that cause amazement), aweful (in the sense of inspiring awe), terrible (in the sense of awakening terror) and over-whelming (in the sense of being beyond our control or manipulation). At other times he appears as gracious, inviting, comforting, enabling and fulfilling. In short, he is the Holy One, the *mysterium tremendum et fascinans*: absolutely terrifying and utterly fascinating.

It comes as little surprise, then, that those who put their trust in such a God will themselves be ambiguous in their stance before him. On the one hand, we want to distance ourselves from him, like Simon Peter who said: 'Depart from me, O Lord, for I am a sinful man' (Luke 5.8). But even as we say this, we also experience that secret longing which the disciples of Emmaus knew so well: 'Stay with us, for it is nearly evening and the day is almost over' (Luke 24.29). Thus our identity as believers is always ambiguous: we are secure and yet homeless, restless seekers and yet the prodigal who has already made it home, 'in the world yet not of the world'.

One would have thought that with the Incarnation, things would have become much clearer, less ambiguous. What we often forget is that incarnation always means more ambiguity – not less! Of all the *magnalia dei*, the great acts of God, surely the Incarnation is by far the one that generates most ambiguity. Human nature is ambiguous in itself. Even St Thomas recognized this when he said: 'In us there is not only the pleasure that we share with the beasts, but also the pleasure we share with the angels.'[5] But when human nature and divine nature are conjoined in a hypostatic union, one has the makings of untold ambiguity.

Let us examine some of the basic ambiguity that surrounded the historical figure of Jesus: how he deliberately created ambiguity, and how he himself experienced it. This will help us to see that ambiguity need not be something which has to be avoided or eliminated at all cost, but can indeed be a divinely-appointed grace, a 'blessing in disguise', a positive invitation to trust in the Lord.

Jesus creates ambiguity

When we focus on the life of Jesus, ambiguity seems to surround him at every turn. Moreover, he was very conscious of this: 'Who do people say that I am?' he asked, and the answers he received varied considerably (Matt. 16.13–16). Those who encountered him felt a basic strangeness in his nature. They do not know quite how they stand with him. Again and again they try to fit him into their ordinary scheme of things, but they never succeed. He strikes them as being too ambiguous – open, that is, to too many possible and even contradictory interpretations.

We see this inherent ambiguity of Jesus, for example, in the way he presented himself to his followers as both master and servant. Jesus is Lord and master – he knows it and says so (Matt. 10.25). Yet he is also one who came 'not to be served by others but to serve' (Matt. 20.28). And even when he tries to remove the distance between himself and his disciples, he nevertheless underlines it, as when he says: 'A servant is no greater than his master. If they persecuted me, they will persecute you too' (John 15, 10). The ambiguity here stems from the fact that he presents himself as absolute master and as absolute servant. He is a servant who remains master and a master who never ceases to be servant. We know that Simon Peter, in particular, had difficulty coping with this ambiguity when Jesus tried to wash his feet (John 13.4–11).

Jesus was being deliberately ambiguous when he told the high priests and elders that even the village prostitutes were further on the road to the Kingdom of God than they were (21.31–32). The Old Testament prophets had often used this image of the prostitute to symbolize Israel's infidelity and estrangement from God. How could prostitutes now be signalled out for commendation? If there was any truth in Jesus' words – even a grain of truth – why wrap it in such ambiguity? Why run counter to the well-established norms and criteria of favour in God's sight? Not only does Jesus reverse the existing identities through the symbol of the prostitute (the righteous becoming the sinners and sinners becoming somehow justified), but he actually calls into question the way in which one's neighbour was hitherto perceived and judged.

Nor can we overlook the ambiguity created by the sort of company Jesus kept and the way he freely associated with women of ill-repute: the notorious sinful woman of the city (Luke 7.36–50), the adulteress (John 8.2–11), the Samaritan woman known to have had six husbands (John 4.5–27), or the one with a longstanding 'flow of blood' (Matt. 5.25–34). Public comportment of this kind was bound to send out 'mixed' signals and give rise to some contentious ambiguity.

Jesus' own tolerance of ambiguity can be seen in the remarkable patience he had with those of his followers who were hesitant and still very tentative in their response to his message. When the Twelve were tempted one day to eliminate some of the existing ambiguity in Jesus' following, he told them the parable of the Weeds (Mark 13.24–30): how the good and the bad must be allowed to live together until the final judgment. By his own reckoning, Jesus' followers would always be an improbable, unseemly, ambiguous lot!

It was not so much *despite* this ambiguity but rather *because of* it that Jesus was able to reveal God's loving patience. What was yesterday's useless weed may become, through grace, tomorrow's fruitful plant. The misfits of society may turn out to be its prophets; today's sinner, tomorrow's saint. Jesus was not one to crush the bruised weed or quench the smouldering wick (Matt. 16.20). He would be patient, but patience, as we know, creates its own ambiguity.

So does deliberate discretion and silence (and our four Gospels attribute a lot of both to Jesus). It is curious and doubtless revealing that Jesus never once on his own took the floor to say who he was. Formal statements concerning his person in the synoptics always come from someone other than he. Moreover Jesus left many questions unanswered and it certainly wasn't for lack of opportunity that he didn't make his positions clearer and less ambiguous. This silence and reserve on the part of Jesus was without doubt a major cause of ambiguity for his contemporaries.

The Gospels give evidence not only that Jesus created ambiguity for others, but that he experienced it himself. It is one of the truly great divine ironies that the very ambiguity which Jesus created through his silence would be visited upon him when the drama of his own life was about to reach its climax.

At Gethsemane and on the cross, Jesus experiences the real agony of ambiguity since it stemmed from the utter silence of precisely the One he had grown accustomed to call 'Abba' – Daddy, dear Father! The God that he had known up to this hour was almighty and all-good, a God who could have chosen for him an entirely different path to arrive at the same goal. Now he appears as the inexorable God of justice. Hence the ambiguity: 'My God, my God, why have you forsaken me?' (Matt. 27.46).

What this great mystery illustrates is that ambiguity, however threatening, harbours a singular grace: it can unleash the most ferocious instincts of fear and abandonment, while at the same time it can expand the souls of those who put their complete and ultimate trust in God. As with Jesus, or Mary, who on more than one occasion exclaimed 'How is this possible?', or Abraham, our father in faith, ambiguity invites us to reach down deeper within ourselves and there, in the 'dark night of the soul', to surrender more completely to the God of Mystery. In short, ambiguity provides the invitation, while the Spirit within gives us the grace to respond.

Thus we come to discern the divine pedagogy of ambiguity, its dynamic pattern and 'inner logic'. The ambiguity that Jesus created stems basically from the dialectic of veiling and unveiling which characterized his humanity. In Jesus, the incarnate Word, God is both unveiled and veiled, manifested but still hidden, self-declared yet not forced upon us with the kind of clarity and overwhelming evidence that would remove all ambiguity – and thus our very freedom. The mystery and deeper reality of Jesus' person is never given as a clear and indisputable fact. Then as now, he reveals himself only in the shadowy light of the human condition and through the 'clair-obscur' of human mediations, symbols that are by nature poly-semic and therefore ambiguous.

In order for Jesus truly to reveal himself, it was not enough to speak clearly or even act decisively: what he said had to be understood and believed. He could not simply say who he was and expect people really to understand him; he could not express the full mystery of his person in any known word or human form of expression. Otherwise we would have been left with just that – *human* concepts and nothing more! Of course he had to use human words and vocabulary to reveal himself, words whose meaning would make some sense to us. But he also had to draw us beyond these human parables and symbols, beyond these finite, human forms of expression. He had to do that so we might surrender to a higher wisdom, a *divine* revelation, and hence something beyond our natural capacity to comprehend.

The only way Jesus could do this was through a pedagogy of ambiguity, that is, by telling us only as much as we needed to know, yet not enough to make us think that he was only communicating human wisdom and not a divine revelation. Thus much of the ambiguity that Jesus created was intended as an *invitation* to explore and probe deeper, to come closer, and be asked that only meaningful and deeply personal question: 'And you, who do *you* say that I am?' Jesus' ambiguity – whether in his words or his actions – always placed the witness in a position in which this question could not be avoided. Only then might the mystery of a divine revelation become effectively received as an invitation, as a personal RSVP, with the real possibility of either surrendering to it or forever being culpable for rejecting it. In short, *ambiguity creates the kind of space necessary for the possibility of faith*.

The ambiguous truth about faith

From everything we have seen thus far, ambiguity can be described as the *climate* of faith, the *condition of its possibility*: neither its ground, nor its goal or perfection, but rather a penultimate means of grace in a world whose final salvation remains an object of hope. For as St Paul says, 'In hope we were saved. But hope is not hope if its object is seen; how is it possible to hope for what one can actually see? But hoping for what we cannot see means awaiting it with patient endurance' (Rom. 8.24–25).

The New Testament writers affirm in various ways that 'we walk by faith, not by sight' (II Cor. 5.7), and that faith only allows us to see 'dimly' or 'indistinctly', as in a mirror (I Cor. 13.12). Thomas Merton the monk would put it this way:

> The very obscurity of faith is an argument of its perfection. It is darkness to our minds because it so far transcends their weakness. The more perfect faith is, the darker it becomes. The closer we get to God, the less is our faith diluted with the half-light of created images and concepts.[6]

Church authorities and church leaders would do well to concede that this describes fairly accurately the actual experience of many believers today – including the many who have taken some distance from external religion and the church as institution. In one of his last essays, the great Karl Rahner wrote: 'The Christian of the future will be a mystic or he will not exist at all.'[7]

This is another way of saying that if the church has been a good teacher, a good *pedagogue*, in the past, she must now become an even better *mystagogue*. And the difference, of course, is crucial. It was Jean Guitton, I believe, who said: 'In the sphere of problems we have to be taught; but in the sphere of mystery we have to be initiated.' The language and discourse of a teacher, for the most part, will be conceptual, rational and logical. It will focus mainly on what can be known, validated and reasonably expressed. The language of a mystagogue, on the other hand, is essentially a language of mystery, a language of the religious imagination, one that invites us to cross over and beyond what meets the eye, beyond what can be known or seen directly – in short, one that initiates us into the Mystery by which 'we live, and move and have our being'.

The ultimate conviction and decision of faith does not come, in the last resort, from a pedagogic indoctrination from outside, even when this is supported by an official teaching of the *magisterium* of the church, but rather from the experience of God, of his spirit, of his freedom, welling up from within and bursting out of the very heart of human existence.

Ambiguity in the early church

Troublesome, disconcerting, and at times pervasive, ambiguity has always been experienced by 'those who have gone before us, marked with the sign of faith'. We might console ourselves by recalling to what extent the early church was plunged into ambiguity as a result of the ongoing delay of the *parousia*, the 'Second Coming'.

What is significant here is that despite their fervent expectation of the imminent return of Jesus in power and glory, the early Christians never allowed the delay of the *parousia* to develop into an acute crisis of faith. Their ambiguity was real, however, and it ran deep! While they became increasingly involved in the day-to-day running and organization of the visible church, they were never quite sure this was the Christian thing to do. Was it not a betrayal of Jesus' promise to return soon? Was it not tantamount to planting shade trees under which the church would never sit?

Throughout this time of uncertainty and ambiguity, no pseudo-clarity was ever forced into the picture. The early church not only learned to live with this ambiguity but, more significantly, it was this very ambiguity that quickened their faith and taught them to renew – on a daily, ongoing basis – their abiding trust and unqualified hope in the Risen Lord.

The delay of the *parousia* certainly raised many questions. But it is precisely because these questions were never stifled, never prematurely foreclosed, never given a final or overly authoritative answer, that sufficient space was created in the church for Christian hope to become contagious. Like the mysterious *manna* that nourished the Israelites in the desert, the early church came to rely on God one day at a time. In this, especially, it proved to be inspired and boldly creative.

In short, it is fitting to recall that God sings some of his best songs in the night, or as Léon Bloy put it: '*Deus dedit carmina in nocte*' ('God gave songs in the night'). From a very tender age, every Christian seems to have known the wonder and truth of this mystery. This is no doubt why the church likes to keep vigil at night especially, and why we continue to chant the venerable words: '*O vere beata nox*' – O truly blessed night! Whether in a stable in Bethlehem or at an empty tomb in Jerusalem, Jesus seems always to have awaited the world at night to hear his Father sing.

Notes

1. K. Rahner, *Theological Investigations* 6, London and New York 1967, 218–30.
2. J. Metz, 'Unbelief as a Theological Problem', *Concilium*, Vol. 6 (June 1969), 59–77.

3. C. J. Jung, *Collected Works* 6, London 1971, 244–5.

4. Augustine, *De bapt.*, V. 27, 28. See also *De civ. Dei*, I.35 and *In Joan. Ev.*, tr. XXVII.11 and tr. XLV.12.

5. Thomas Aquinas, *Summa theologica*, I–II, 31, 4 ad 3.

6. Thomas Merton, *New Seeds of Contemplation*, New York 1961, 134.

7. K. Rahner, *Concerns for the Church*, New York 1981, 149.

Contributors

CHRISTIAN DUQUOC was born in Nantes, France, in 1926 and ordained priest in 1953. He studied at the Dominican house of Leysse, France; the university of Fribourg, Switzerland; at Le Saulchoir, Paris; and the Ecole Biblique in Jerusalem, gaining a doctorate in theology. He is editor of the journal *Lumière et Vie*; his publications include *Christologie* (2 vols.), Paris 1972; *Jesus, homme libre*, Paris 1973; *Dieu différent*, Paris 1977; *Messianisme de Jésus et discretion de Dieu*, Geneva 1984; *Provisional Churches*, London 1986; *Liberation et Progressisme*, Paris 1987.

Address: 2 Place Gailleton, 69002 Lyons, France

ERHARD S. GERSTENBERGER was born in 1932, a miner's son in the Ruhr. He studied Protestant theology from 1952–1957, and from 1959–1964 was a student and lecturer at Yale Divinity School, USA. After ten years as a parish minister in Essen, he lectured in São Leopoldo, Brazil, from 1975 to 1981, when he became Professor of Old Testament in Giessen. Since then he has been Professor at the Philipps-Universität, Marburg. He is married with three children and his books include: *Der bittende Mensch. Bittritual und Klagelied des Einzelnen*, Neukirchen-Vlyun 1980; *Suffering*, Nashville 1980; *Woman and Man*, Nashville 1982; *Jahwe-ein patriarchaler Gott*, Stuttgart, 1988; *Psalms, Part I, with an Introduction to Cultic Poetry*, FOTL XIV/1, Grand Rapids 1988.

Address: Fasanenweg 29, D6300 Giessen, Germany

GREGORY BAUM was born in Berlin in 1923; since 1940 he has lived in Canada. He studied at McMaster University, Hamilton; Ohio State University; the University of Fribourg and the New School for Social Research, New York. He is now Professor of Theology and Social Ethics at McGill University, Montreal. He is editor of *The Ecumenist*; his books include *Religion and Alienation* (1975), *The Social Imperative* (1978), *Catholics and Canadian Socialism* (1980), *The Priority of Labor* (1982), *Ethics and Economics* (1984) and *Theology and Society* (1987).

Address: McGill University, 3520 University St, Montreal H3A 2A7

PABLO RICHARD was born in Chile in 1939. He gained a licentiate in theology in 1966 from the Universidad Católica de Chile, a licentiate in sacred scripture in 1969 from the Pontifical Biblical Institute in Rome and a doctorate in sociology of religion in 1978 from the Sorbonne in Paris, and was also awarded an honorary doctorate in theology from the Faculté Livre de Théologie Protestante in Paris. He lives now in Costa Rica, where he is titular professor of theology in the National University and a member of DEI (Ecumenical Research Department), which is dedicated to the continuing formation of pastoral workers for ecclesial base communities in popular environments in Central America. His latest books are *La Iglesia latinoamericana entre el temor y la esperanza*, San José 1987, and *Death of Christendoms, Birth of the Church*, Maryknoll, NY 1988.

Address: Departmento Ecomenico de Investigaciones, Apartado Postal 389 – Sabarilla, 2070 San José, Costa Rica

ANDRÉS TORNOS gained doctorates in theology from the University of Innsbruck (1959) and philosophy from the University of Munich (1960). He studied clinical psychology in Madrid and gained a diploma in 1963. For twelve years he taught philosophical anthropology in Madrid, and was visiting lecturer in Buenos Aires, Lima, Santiago de Chile and Kinshasa. Since 1973 he has been Professor of Eschatology in the Comillas University in Madrid, as well as carrying out research in the sociology of religion in the Comillas Institute for Faith and Secularity. His recent publications include *Escatología I* (1989), *Escatología II* (1991), and a study of guilt in *Psicología y Ejercicios Ignacianos*, vol. I (1991).

Address: Universidad Comillas, 28049 Madrid, Spain

PIERRE DE LOCHT was born in Brussels in 1916 and ordained priest in 1940; he has a doctorate in theology from the University of Louvain. Since 1946 he has been involved in pastoral work with families (marriage preparation, house groups, marriage guidance counselling). In 1957/58 he was professor of moral theology in the Lovanium faculty of theology, Zaire. From 1967 he was senior lecturer at the University of Louvain, teaching at the Institut des sciences familiales et sexologiques. He is now retired. In addition to articles on morals and especially sexuality, he has written: *A la mésure de son Amour*, Paris 1961; *Harmonie des vocations*, Tournai 1965; *La morale conjugale en recherche*, Tournai 1968; *Et pourtant je crois*, Tournai 1970; *Les risques de la fidelité*, Paris 1972; *Les couples et l'église: chronique d'un témoin*, Paris 1979; *J'espère être croyant, itineraire d'un croyant*, Paris 1981; *Pour une approche plus sereine . . . à propos de l'avortement*, Brussels 1982; *L'avortement, les enjeux d'un débat passioné*, Brussels 1985.

Address: 58, rue de la Prévoyance, B 1000 Brussels, Belgium

YVES CATTIN is Associate Professor of Philosophy in the Philosophy Department of the Blaise Pascal University of Clermont-Ferrand, France. In addition to numerous articles on philosophy, he has written two books: *La preuve de Dieu*, Paris 1987; *Court traité de l'existence chrétienne*, Paris 1992.

Address: Saignes, F 63710 Saint Nectaire, France

ISABELLE CHAREIRE was born in 1957 at Annonay, France. Having gained a diploma in further studies in theology and philosophy, she is now working towards a doctoral thesis. She has already written several articles, published in *Concilium* and in *Lumière et Vie*.

Address: 164 rue Paul-Bert, 69003 Lyons, France

JOSÉ-IGNACIO GONZÁLEZ-FAUS SJ was born in Valencia in 1933 and ordained in 1963. He is Professor of Systematic Theology in the Faculty of Catalonia. From 1969 to 1977 he edited the journal *Selecciones de Teología*. He is the Director of the theological area in the Cristianismo y Justicia study centre, and gives regular courses in the Central American University (San Salvador) and in the CRT in Mexico. Among his recent publications are *Where the Spirit Breathes. Prophetic Dissent in the Church*, Maryknoll, NY 1989, and *Vicarios de Cristo, Los pobres en la teología y espiritualidad cristiana*, Madrid 1991.

Address: Centre Borja, Llaseres 30, 08190 Sant Cugat del Vallès, Barcelona, Spain

RICHARD G. COTE OMI was born at Lewiston, USA in 1934. He studied at the universities of Angers and Strasbourg, gaining his doctorate in theology in 1967. He has worked in Southern Africa for fifteen years, mainly in the teaching field of higher education and theology. He is now Associate Professor at Loyola University, New Orleans. His published works include *Could It Be?* and *Universal Grace: Myth or Reality?*

Address: St Paul University, 223 Main Street, Ottawa, Ontario K1S 1C4, Canada.

Members of the Advisory Committee for Spirituality

Directors

Christian Duquoc OP	Lyons	France
Casiano Florestán	Madrid	Spain

Members

Frei Betto	Sao Paulo	Brazil
Enzo Bianchi	Magnano	Italy
Carlo Carozzo	Genoa	Italy
Johannes van Galen, OCarm	Aalsmeer	Netherlands
Michel de Goedt OCD	Paris	France
Gustavo Gutiérrez	Lima	Peru
Ernest Larkin, OCarm	Phoenix, AZ	USA
Jean Leclercq OSB	Clervaux	Luxembourg
Pierre de Locht	Brussels	Belgium
Edward Malatesta SJ	San Francisco, CA	USA
Maria Martinell	Barcelona	Spain
Jan Peters OCD	Geysteren	Netherlands
Samuel Rayan SJ	Delhi	India
Samuel Ruiz	Chiapas	Mexico
Jean-Claude Sagne OP	Lyons	France
Charles Schleck CSC	Rome	Italy
Pedro Trigo	Caracas	Venezuela
Fernando de Urbina	Madrid	Spain

Concilium

Issues of *Concilium* to be published in 1993

Messianism through History

Edited by Wim Beuken, Sean Freyne and Anton Weiler

Explores the role that the notion of a Messiah has played in determining Jewish and Christian self-identities through history. After a first section on the latest understanding of the biblical background it traces messianic thought in Judaism and Christianity in the Middle Ages before discussing the implications of messianic belief today.

03018 8   1993/1   February

Any Room for Christ in Asia?

Edited by Leonardo Boff and Virgil Elizondo in collaboration with Aloysius Pieris and Mary-John Mananzan

In Asia, Christians are a very small percentage of the people. Is this inevitable? A first section looks at the guises in which 'Christ' entered Asia and non-Christian perceptions of Christ; this is followed by accounts of specific current theological interpretations of Christ in Asian churches.

03019 6   1993/2   April

The Spectre of Mass Death

Edited by David N. Power

How does Christianity repond to catastrophes involving the sudden deaths of thousands: war, famine and flood or epidemics like AIDS and drugs? This issue begins with examples of how people do in fact react, considers traditional responses to the question of evil in this connection, and then considers possible liturgical remembrance and forms of prayer.

03020 X   1993/3   June

Reincarnation or Resurrection?

Edited by Hermann Häring and Johann-Baptist Metz

A first part considers varieties of ideas of reincarnation in Hinduism, Buddhism, Latin America and African religion, and the popularity of reincarnation in modern belief; a second part adopts a similar approach to ideas of resurrection; the final part compares and contrasts the two approaches.

03021 8   1993/4   August

Migrants and Refugees

Edited by Norbert Greinacher and Norbert Mette

The mass migration of people, especially in the Third World, as a result of war, famine or other pressures, is a major problem for the world. This issue offers accounts of what is actually happening on various continents, analyses the sociology of migration, considers the ethical issues and outlines possible Christian responses.

03022 6   1993/5   October

Mass Media

Edited by John A. Coleman and Miklos Tomka

This issue recognizes that the media represent a complex phenomenon requiring deeper analysis than the church is often prepared to give. It seeks to help readers to understand better how the media work, how media communication should be 'read' and the moral and value issues involved in debates on the media.

03023 4   1993/6   December

Titles for Issues to be Published in 1994

No increase in subscriptions for 1993

We are pleased to announce that there will be no increase in subscriptions for 1993.

Back Issues of Concilium still available

All listed issues are available at £6.95/US$15.00 each. Add 10% of value for postage.
Special rates are sometimes available for large orders. Please write for details.

1965

1	Dogma ed. Schillebeeckx: *The very first issue*
2	Liturgy On the Vatican Constitution: *Jungmann and Gelineau*
3	Pastoral ed. Rahner: *The first issue on this topic*
4	Ecumenism: *Küng on charismatic structure, Baum on other churches*
5	Moral Theology: *Its nature: law, decalogue, birth control*
6	Church and World: *Metz, von Balthasar, Rahner on ideology*
7	Church History: *Early church, Constance, Trent, religious freedom*
8	Canon Law: *Conferences and Collegiality*
9	Spirituality: *Murray Rogers, von Balthasar: East and West*
10	Scripture Inspiration and Authority; *R.E. Murphy, Bruce Vawter*

1966

11	Dogma Christology: *Congar, Schoonenberg, Vorgrimler*
12	Liturgy: *The liturgical assembly, new church music*
13	Pastoral Mission after Vatican 2
14	Ecumenism: *Getting to know the other churches*
15	Moral Theology Religious Freedom: *Roland Bainton, Yves Congar*
16	Church and World Christian Faith v. Atheism: *Moltmann, Ricoeur*
17	Church History: *Jansenism, Luther, Gregorian Reform*
18	Religious Freedom In Judaism, Hinduism, Spain, Africa
19	Religionless Christianity? *Bernard Cooke, Duquoc, Geffre*
20	Bible and Tradition: *Blenkinsopp, Fitzmeyer, P. Grelot*

1967

21	Revelation and Dogma: *A reconsideration*
23	Atheism and Indifference: *Includes two Rahner articles*
24	Debate on the Sacraments: *Thurian, Kasper, Ratzinger, Meyendorff*
25	Morality, Progress and History: *Can the moral law develop?*
26	Evolution: *Harvey Cox, Ellul, Rahner, Eric Mascall*
27	Church History: *Sherwin-White and Oberman; enlightenment*
28	Canon Law - Theology and Renewal: *Hopes for the new Canon Law*
29	Spirituality and Politics: *Balthasar; J.A.T. Robinson discussed*
30	The Value of the OT: *John McKenzie, Munoz Iglesias, Coppens*

1968

31	Man, World and Sacrament: *Congar, J.J.Hughes on Anglican orders*
32	Death and Burial: *Theology and Liturgy*
33	Preaching the Word of God: *Congar, Rahner on demythologizing*
34	Apostolic by Succession? *Issues in ministry*
35	The Church and Social Morality: *Major article by Garaudy*
36	Faith and Politics: *Metz, Schillebeeckx, Leslie Dewart*
37	Prophecy: *Francis of Assisi, Ignatius of Loyola, Wesley, Newman*
38	Order and the Sacraments: *Confirmation, marriage, bishops*

Please send remittances and any enquiries to:

SCM Press Ltd, 26-30 Tottenham Road, London N1 4BZ

Published by SCM Press in June 1992

The Body in Context

Sex and Catholicism

Gareth Moore OP

In this important new book, Gareth Moore examines some of the principal arguments and styles of arguments which Christians, and particularly the Roman Catholic Church, have advanced in support of Christian standards in sexual ethics.

Catholic teaching has sought to present Christian sexual standards and values as reasonable, as standards which anyone can see to be right if only they think about them in the right way. Arguments have been drawn from both scripture and from philosophy and experience, the latter being particularly important at a time when the church can no longer lay down the law, but has to be able to persuade.

However, are the arguments used valid, or are they flawed? This is what Gareth Moore considers. His study covers such wide-ranging topics as sexual pleasure, the purpose of sex, sexual gestures, marriage, contraception and homosexuality, and in these areas, and the more specific sexual issues which he covers, he often finds the church's case defective. Though the church has many valuable things to say, its supporting arguments can be unconvincing.

Better arguments, he claims, are needed, or alternatively the possibility has to be faced that the church's teaching needs to be modified. But it does need to do more thinking about sex.

Gareth Moore OP is a member of the Dominican Order and teaches at Blackfriars, Oxford.

0 334 02525 7   paper   £17.50

Concilium Subscription Information

Individual Annual Subscription (six issues): £30.00/US$50.00
Institution Annual Subscription (six issues): £40.00/US$75.00
Airmail subscriptions: add £10.00/US$25.00
Individual issues: £8.95/US$15.00 each

New subscribers please return this form:
for a two-year subscription, double the appropriate rate

(for individuals)   £30.00/US$50.00   (1/2 years) . . . .

(for institutions)   £40.00/US$75.00   (1/2 years) . . . .

Airmail postage outside Europe and
USA   +£10.00/US$25.00 (1/2 years) . . . .

Total . . . . . .

I wish to subscribe for one/two years as an individual/institution
(delete as appropriate)

Name/Institution . . . .

Address . . . .

. . . .

. . . .

I enclose a cheque for . . . . payable to SCM Press Ltd

Please charge my Access/Visa/Mastercard no. . . . .

Signature . . . . .Expiry Date . . . .

Please return this form to:
SCM PRESS LTD 26-30 Tottenham Road, London N1 4BZ